AMERICA the BEAUTIFUL
PUERTO RICO

By Deborah Kent

Consultants

José Antonio Pérez Ruiz, Associate Professor of History, University of Puerto Rico

Robert L. Hillerich, Ph.D., Bowling Green State University, Bowling Green, Ohio

CHILDRENS PRESS®
CHICAGO

A fruit stand in Old San Juan

Project Editor: Joan Downing
Associate Editor: Shari Joffe
Design Director: Margrit Fiddle
Typesetting: Graphic Connections, Inc.
Engraving: Liberty Photoengraving

Library of Congress Cataloging-in-Publication Data

Kent, Deborah.
    America the beautiful. Puerto Rico / by Deborah
Kent.
        p.   cm.
    Includes index.
    Summary: Introduces the geography, people,
history, and culture of this island.
    ISBN 0-516-00498-0
    1.   Puerto Rico—Juvenile literature.
[1.   Puerto Rico]   I.   Title.
F1958.3.K4   1991   91-543
972.95—dc20   CIP
                                               AC

Participants in a festival in Ponce

TABLE OF CONTENTS

Chapter 1
WELCOME TO PUERTO RICO

WELCOME TO PUERTO RICO

The Condado district of Puerto Rico's capital, San Juan, is a modern landscape of high-rise hotels and apartment complexes. Well-dressed shoppers and office workers hurry along the crowded sidewalks. With its glass and steel, its snarling traffic, and its jarring pace, the Condado has the flavor of any bustling city in the United States.

Perched on a promontory at the eastern edge of the Condado is El Viejo San Juan, Old San Juan. Here, wrought-iron balconies and steeples of ancient churches overlook a network of twisting cobbled streets laid more than three centuries ago. Old men play dominoes in quiet plazas and friends visit in open-air cafes. The United States seems far away, edged aside by a flourishing legacy from old Spain.

Both Spain and the United States have contributed to the character of Puerto Rico. The two traditions—Spanish and North American—are powerful forces in Puerto Rican society today. To these ingredients the Puerto Rican people have added the spices of the Caribbean, creating a culture that is truly their own.

Natives of the Commonwealth of Puerto Rico are American citizens, yet Spanish is their native language. Politically and economically, Puerto Rico is closely tied to the United States, yet the island is often seen as a model for Latin American development. Puerto Rico is not an independent nation, yet it has its own flag, its own anthem, and its own Olympic team.

As the twenty-first century approaches, Puerto Rico faces a host of challenges. These will surely be met by a people who speak with pride of their island home as *la patria*, "the fatherland."

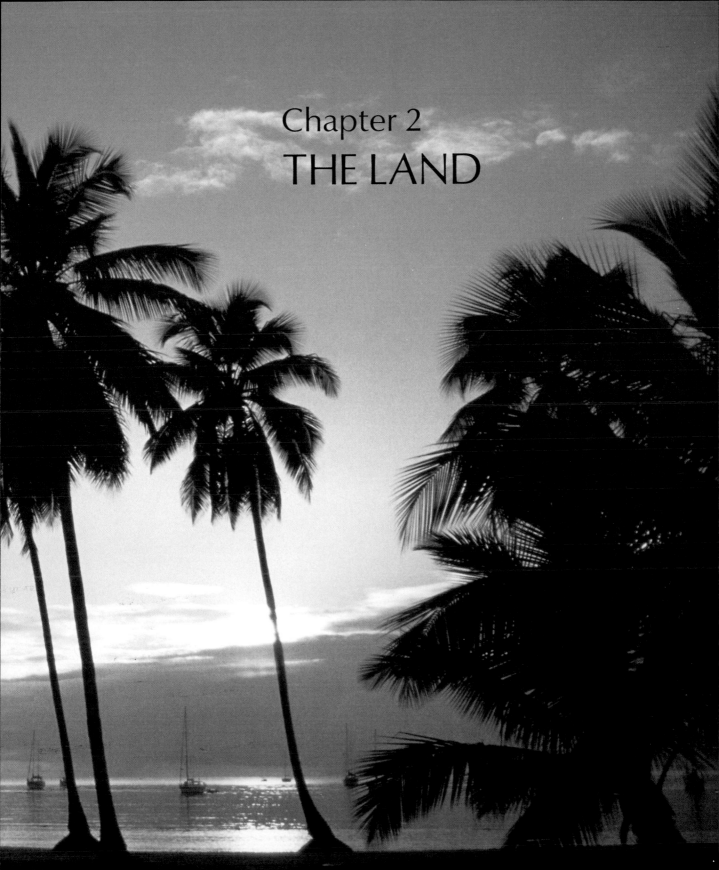

Chapter 2
THE LAND

THE LAND

GEOGRAPHY

Puerto Rico is an island located about 1,000 miles (1,609 kilometers) southeast of Florida's southern tip. It belongs to the archipelago, or group of islands, known as the West Indies or Antilles. Covering 3,515 square miles (9,104 square kilometers), Puerto Rico is about the size of the state of Connecticut.

The West Indian archipelago spreads in a vast arc through the Caribbean Basin, from Florida almost to the coast of Venezuela. According to geologists, the Antilles are actually the peaks of mountains that have been submerged for millions of years. If the seawater were drained away, these mountains would be taller than the Himalayas of Nepal.

Puerto Rico is the easternmost island in the West Indian chain known as the Greater Antilles. Other islands in this chain include Cuba, Jamaica, and Hispaniola (shared by the nations of Haiti and the Dominican Republic). The northern coast of Puerto Rico faces the Atlantic Ocean, while the coasts to the south and east are lapped by the Caribbean Sea. The Dominican Republic is Puerto Rico's western neighbor across Mona Passage.

Three offshore islands and several tiny dots of land, called keys, are considered part of Puerto Rico. The largest of these offshore islands is Vieques, which lies to the east and covers about 57 square miles (148 square kilometers). Vieques is used by the United States Navy for maneuvers and as a target range. Nearby is

Vieques is one of Puerto Rico's offshore islands.

the island of Culebra. Mona, 42 miles (68 kilometers) west of Puerto Rico, is a sanctuary for nesting and migrating seabirds.

Puerto Rico is roughly rectangular in shape, scored by a series of steep mountain ridges and deep, narrow valleys. About three-fourths of the island's terrain is hilly or mountainous. The Cordillera Central, Puerto Rico's chief mountain range, runs like a spine across the length of the island from east to west. The highest peak on the island is Cerro de Punta, which rises 4,389 feet (1,338 meters) above sea level. El Yunque, a famous, rain-forest-covered peak whose name means "the anvil," is part of the Sierra de Luquillo range at the eastern end of the island.

Along the Atlantic coast stretches a narrow strip of lowland called the North Coast Plain. Here lie many of Puerto Rico's most

Puerto Rico's terrain includes lush mountains (left) and beaches lined with towering cliffs (right).

popular beaches, as well as San Juan, the island's capital and largest city. The coastal plain on the Caribbean side of the island is even narrower, rising abruptly to rugged mountain peaks.

LAKES, LAGOONS, AND RIVERS

Puerto Rico has few freshwater lakes or ponds. Sixteen artificial lakes, however, have been created during the twentieth century to provide water for irrigation. These include Lakes Cidra, Guajataca, and Caonillas. Many of these lakes are stocked with catfish, bass, and other game fish.

The 311-mile (500-kilometer) coastline of Puerto Rico is stippled with a series of brackish inlets and lagoons. The largest

The seacoast at Cabo Rojo

and most important of these is San Juan Bay, which offers an excellent harbor on the Atlantic coast. Among the smaller lagoons are San Jose, at the Víedras River; Guánica, near the town of Guánica; and Joyuda, north of Cabo Rojo.

Heavy rainfall and steep mountains have blessed Puerto Rico with a myriad of tumbling streams and rivers. Some mountain streams have carved underground tunnels through the hills, riddling the island with a labyrinth of caves. None of the island's rivers are deep enough to be navigated by oceangoing ships. But these waterways are a vital resource on the island, irrigating fields and generating hydroelectric power.

Puerto Rico's swiftest rivers flow north down the Cordillera Central to empty into the Atlantic. The Plata River runs for 46

The Cordillera Central is Puerto Rico's mountainous "backbone."

miles (74 kilometers) from Cayey to Dorado. At the mouth of the Loíza, east of San Juan, sparkles Luquillo Beach, one of Puerto Rico's most popular resorts. Other rivers on the island include the Río Grande de Bayamón and the Río Grande de Arecibo.

PLANT AND ANIMAL LIFE

In the middle of the nineteenth century, about three-fourths of Puerto Rico was covered with tropical forest. Due to the pressures of an ever-increasing population, only about 25 percent of the land remains forested today.

Tiny as it is, Puerto Rico supports an astonishing variety of vegetation. Scientists have identified some 3,355 species of trees, shrubs, and plants that grow on the island. In the rain forest of El Yunque—part of the Caribbean National Forest—stand giant ferns 20 to 30 feet (6 to 9 meters) tall. Dazzling orchids cling to

Abundant rainfall nourishes the mountainside rain forest known as El Yunque.

the branches of palm, ebony, and sandalwood trees. In dramatic contrast, the southern coast of the island resembles the southwestern United States, with spiny cacti and a scattering of drought-resistant trees.

Some Puerto Rican flora can be found nowhere else in the world. The spectacular violet tree is festooned with purple blossoms every spring. The wood of the prized *ausubo* tree, now nearly extinct, is so hard that it can chip an ax blade. When old houses are demolished, the *ausubo* beams are often saved by historical societies to be used in restoration projects.

Many of the trees and plants common in Puerto Rico today are not really native to the island, but were introduced by Europeans from other parts of the globe. The *flamboyán* (royal poinciana), whose red blossoms blaze along roadsides during the summer months, is actually a transplant from Madagascar. Coconut palms

Puerto Rico's landscape is brightened by such flora and fauna
as the exotic flowers of the Indian banana tree (top left),
brilliant pink bougainvillea blossoms (top right), darting anole
lizards (bottom left), and colorful butterflies (bottom right).

came to Puerto Rico from the Cape Verde Islands. Even such tropical staples as orange and lemon trees did not grow in Puerto Rico when Columbus arrived, but were brought later by the Spanish colonists.

Puerto Rico's largest mammal, the mongoose, is also a relative newcomer to the island. This weasel-like carnivore was introduced from Asia to help kill rats. Unfortunately, mongooses also like to eat chickens and have done untold damage to the island's poultry.

Several species of bats colonize the caves on the island and perform a vital service by devouring millions of mosquitoes every year. The dung of these bats, called *güano,* is an excellent fertilizer.

Puerto Rico is a bird-watcher's paradise. Some two hundred bird species nest or winter on the island. The tiny sugar-bird, or *reinita,* meaning "little queen," sometimes flies boldly through open kitchen windows to steal honey or jam from the table. Hummingbirds flit like winged jewels among garden flowers. The rare, colorful Puerto Rican parrot fights for survival in El Yunque. Many kinds of ducks, sandpipers, terns, and plovers breed along the shore.

Even in San Juan, small lizards are often seen darting through shrubbery or scampering along fences. Iguanas live on the island of Mona. Puerto Rico has several species of snakes, none of them poisonous. The largest, the Puerto Rican boa, can grow up to 7 feet (2 meters) long. The only dangerous creature on the island is a huge centipede whose bite can cause severe illness and even death. Workers in the sugarcane fields, where this insect often lurks, are careful to tuck their trousers into the tops of their boots for protection.

Probably no creature is dearer to the Puerto Rican heart than the tiny frog known as the *coquí.* The *coquí* is named for its high,

The fiery red blossoms of the _flamboyán_ are a familiar sight in Puerto Rico.

clear song of two rising notes, which rings from gardens and woodlands throughout the island. After sundown, the chorus of _coquís_ is part of the Puerto Rican landscape.

CLIMATE

There is a saying in Puerto Rico that if the avocado crop is good, the island will be spared from hurricanes. Most of the time, tropical storms miss Puerto Rico altogether or merely ruffle it with a bit of wind and heavy rain. Every few years, however, a hurricane strikes with vicious force. In 1989, Hurricane Hugo raked across the eastern end of the island, leaving some twenty-eight thousand people homeless.

In general, Puerto Rico basks in glowing sunshine. Though the island receives an average of 77 inches (196 centimeters) of rain

Puerto Rico's year-round sunny weather allows residents to take advantage of the island's many beautiful beaches.

annually, most of it comes in the form of quick showers that are hardly an inconvenience. The rain forest of El Yunque receives about sixteen hundred such showers in the course of a year.

Rainfall is heaviest in the northern part of the island, which receives about 70 inches (178 centimeters) of precipitation a year. The south averages 37 inches (94 centimeters) of rain per year. Droughts in this region can be severe, and the vegetation has adapted to the irregular water supply.

Puerto Rico's climate is mild year-round, and snowfall is unknown. The coldest temperature ever recorded on the island was 40 degrees Fahrenheit (4 degrees Celsius), at Aibonito on March 9, 1911. The annual mean temperature on the island is 76 degrees Fahrenheit (24 degrees Celsius), and temperatures rarely fall below 60 degrees Fahrenheit (16 degrees Celsius). The island's highest reading, recorded at San Lorenzo on August 22, 1906, was 103 degrees Fahrenheit (39 degrees Celsius).

Chapter 3
THE PEOPLE

THE PEOPLE

According to the 1980 federal census, the island of Puerto Rico is home to 3,196,520 people. An average of 909 people crowd each square mile (351 people for each square kilometer) of land area. In contrast, the United States as a whole averages only 67 people per square mile (26 people per square kilometer). If the United States were as densely populated as Puerto Rico, it would have to find room for nearly 3 billion people—almost as many as inhabit the entire earth. Puerto Rico's population growth has been relatively sudden. Since 1898, the number of people on the island has tripled. Preliminary 1990 census figures indicate that the population has grown to 3.5 million.

Puerto Rico is predominantly an urban society, with 67 percent of its people living in cities and towns. Half of Puerto Rico's city dwellers live along the north coast. San Juan, Puerto Rico's capital, is the biggest city on the island, as well as its most important industrial and cultural center. Puerto Rico's second-largest city, Bayamón, lies within the San Juan metropolitan area. Ponce, on the south coast, and Mayagüez, in the west, are both major shipping ports. Caguas, in the hills 22 miles (35 kilometers) south of San Juan, is Puerto Rico's largest inland city.

WHO ARE THE PUERTO RICANS?

The people of Puerto Rico love festivals. Nearly every town has a patron saint and celebrates its special saint's day with parades

Schoolchildren in San Juan

and fireworks. As the floats roll down the streets of San Lorenzo or Jayuya, cheering crowds throng the sidewalks. Some of the spectators have pale, European faces. Others are dark-skinned with African features. And many are of a soft tan hue that Puerto Ricans call *trigueño*.

Puerto Rico is one of the world's true ethnic mosaics, a place where many peoples have blended smoothly and peaceably together. In many Latin American countries, people identify themselves as Spanish, Indian, or mestizo (of mixed blood). In Puerto Rico, however, people seldom rely on such distinctions. First and foremost, they regard themselves as Puerto Ricans.

Most islanders are descended at least in part from the Spanish colonists who controlled Puerto Rico for nearly four centuries.

Puerto Ricans celebrate their heritage by holding colorful festivals (left) and by preserving time-honored religious traditions (right).

Unlike the British, who colonized much of North America, the Spaniards freely intermarried with people of other races. They soon mingled with Puerto Rico's Native American people, the Taínos (also called the Arawaks), and with the African people who were brought as slaves to work on the island's sugarcane plantations.

During the nineteenth century, people from all over the world added their unique flavors to the Puerto Rican stew. Chinese laborers came to build roads and stayed to make the island their home. Italian and Lebanese communities sprang up, eventually assimilating into the larger society. After 1898, people from the United States, or *continentales*, began moving to Puerto Rico.

In addition, since the early 1800s, Puerto Rico has been a haven for refugees from war-torn Latin American nations. Venezuelans and exiles from the Dominican Republic were among those who have built new lives in Puerto Rico when military coups wracked their homelands.

RELIGION

Roman Catholicism runs like a powerful undercurrent through nearly every aspect of Puerto Rican life. When a new store opens in San Juan, the owner often invites a priest to bless the business. When two friends make plans to meet on Thursday, one of them may add, *"Si Dios quiere,"* "If God wills."

About 85 percent of Puerto Ricans are members of the Catholic church. Baptist, Methodist, Lutheran, and Episcopalian congregations also meet in many cities. In recent decades, Evangelical Protestant sects have gained popularity in Puerto Rico, as they have in Central America and the Dominican Republic.

Though most Puerto Ricans are Christians, many also practice *espiritismo*, or spiritualism, a blend of Indian, African, and Catholic beliefs. Followers of *espiritismo* feel that events are controlled by good and evil spirits that can be encouraged or warded off with the proper herbs and rituals. Spiritualism has gradually declined in urban areas. But many Puerto Ricans admit that, though they do not practice spiritualism, they respect it.

POLITICS

The majority of Puerto Ricans are happy with the island's status as a commonwealth of the United States. But others feel that this status is ambiguous and unacceptable. The people who reject the status quo are sharply divided between those who want Puerto Rico to become a full-fledged American state, and those who wish to see the island gain complete independence.

At election time, the island's status is the overriding issue for its political parties. The Popular Democrats favor commonwealth status, which has existed since 1952. The New Progressive party favors statehood, and members of the Puerto Rican Independence party want Puerto Rico to become a sovereign nation.

Since the 1950s, the Popular Democratic party (PDP) has dominated the political scene on the island. The New Progressive party is smaller but has grown steadily. In most elections, the Independence party receives only a fraction of the vote. Yet the independence movement has attracted some of Puerto Rico's leading writers, artists, and scholars. The *Independistas* may be few in number, but they are eloquent and full of passion for their cause.

LANGUAGE

Most Puerto Ricans are of Spanish descent, and Spanish is the language heard everywhere on the island. After 1898, the United States strongly encouraged the use of English, but the Puerto Rican people clung steadfastly to the Spanish language as an integral part of their heritage. Today, Spanish is Puerto Rico's first language, and English is taught as a second language in the schools. Most people in the cities have some knowledge of English for business purposes.

Due to the free flow of people between Puerto Rico and the United States mainland, Puerto Rican Spanish has absorbed many English words. An elevator is called an *elevador*, and the grassy

A fisherman casting his net

space behind a house is known as the *yarda*. At the same time, however, Spanish prevails over many American terms. Though Puerto Rico uses American currency, people on the island generally call a penny a *centavo* and a dollar a *peso*.

Spanish surnames can be confusing to people unfamiliar with the language. A Puerto Rican uses the surnames of both parents, the father's name coming first. Thus, the father of Puerto Rican patriot Luis Muñoz Rivera was a Muñoz, while his mother was a Rivera. Muñoz Rivera's son retained the Muñoz but dropped the Rivera in exchange for his mother's father's name, Marín—thus he was known as Luis Muñoz Marín. When a woman marries, she drops her mother's family name and adds the first surname of her husband. Thus, if Carmen Morales Rivera marries Enrique Guzman Robles, she becomes Carmen Morales de Guzman.

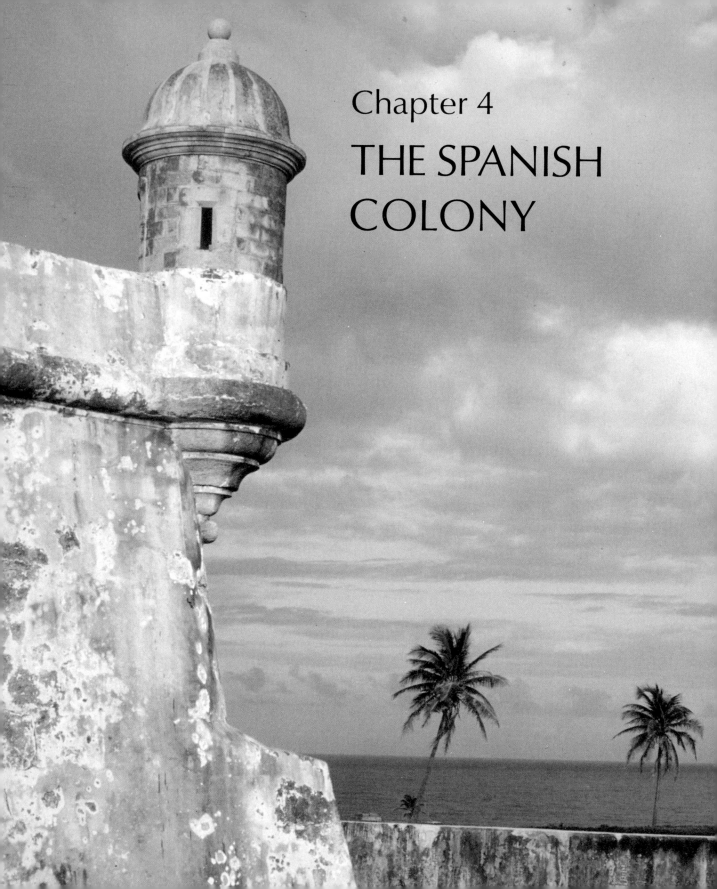

Chapter 4
THE SPANISH
COLONY

THE SPANISH COLONY

"[The fortress] standeth in a good situation, and in a convenient place on a high mount which doth lie upon the entering in of the harbor. . . . When it is completed, it will be the strongest that His Majesty hath in all the Indies, and now the people of the country sleep in security." So wrote Puerto Rico's colonial governor, Diego Menéndez de Valdés, to the King of Spain in 1590. With its strategic position at the mouth of the Caribbean, Puerto Rico promised Spain tremendous military advantages. But the first centuries as a Spanish colony proved more arduous than the early explorers and settlers could have imagined.

THE PEOPLE OF BORINQUÉN

Puerto Rico's first inhabitants, who arrived between five thousand and twenty thousand years ago, probably reached the island by boat from Florida and Cuba. Today known simply as the Archaics, they were the descendants of wandering Asian peoples who had crossed into North America thousands of years before. They fished and gathered wild fruits, and never stayed in one place for long.

In 1948, a team led by archaeologist Ricardo Alegría discovered some ancient stone tools in a cave near Loíza Aldea on Puerto Rico's northeastern coast. These artifacts were left behind by a later wave of migrants who spread to the West Indies from the South American mainland about two thousand years ago. Referred to by archaeologists as the Igneri, these people were

Above: Examples of ancient Igneri pottery
Right: A young man portraying a Taíno Indian
during the Festival Indigena in Jayuya

among several related groups known collectively as the Arawak.
The Arawak used clay to make bowls and cups. Many of their
villages had walled courts where the young men played
ceremonial games with a rubber ball.

The Taínos, an Arawak people who reached Puerto Rico around
A.D. 1000, eventually became the dominant group on the island.
The Taínos were a peace-loving people who lived in villages. Each
village was ruled by a *cacique*, or chief. These lesser chiefs were
united under a single *cacique* who ruled the entire island in the
event of war. The Taínos believed in a supreme being who had
created the world and ruled over many lesser gods. The English
word *hurricane* comes from *Jurakán*, the Taíno name for their god
of destructive winds.

Swift Taíno canoes carried traders from one island to another
throughout the Antilles. To the Taínos, the island we now call
Puerto Rico was *Borinquén*, "land of the brave lord."

By the 1400s, the peaceful Taínos were under attack from the Caribs, a new group that migrated to the islands from South America. The dreaded Caribs were a warlike tribe, known to feast on captives taken in battle. But the Taínos soon faced an enemy who would spread even greater devastation than the Caribs could devise.

SAN JUAN BAUTISTA

Early in 1493, a sea captain named Christopher Columbus arrived at the palace of King Ferdinand and Queen Isabella of Spain. Columbus was laden with gifts and bursting with pride. He had sailed west across the Atlantic Ocean and, just as he had promised, he had found India—or at least a cluster of islands off the Indian coast. His sea route to the Orient would surely make Spain the richest nation on earth.

The king and queen were thrilled by Columbus's news. When Columbus had set out on his first voyage westward, the king and queen had given him only three tiny ships. Now they ordered him to make a second voyage of exploration, this time with seventeen ships and fifteen hundred men—sailors, mapmakers, priests, artisans, and soldiers. He would claim all the wondrous new lands across the sea for the Spanish Crown.

However, Columbus had not discovered a route to India at all, but had sailed into the Caribbean and blundered into the Antilles Islands. On his second voyage, he again made his way from one island to another, searching for Oriental riches. On one of the islands he visited, he found twelve Taíno women and two boys who had been captured by the Caribs. Columbus took them on board and agreed to carry them back home. They said they lived on the island of Borinquén.

For days, Columbus's fleet threaded its way through narrow channels among coral reefs and tiny keys. At last, the watchmen sighted an island larger than the rest. With cries of joy, the Taíno captives sprang overboard and swam to shore. They were safely home at last.

The Spanish fleet made its way along the island's southern coast. On November 19, Columbus dropped anchor in a bay and went ashore. The expedition found a Taíno village, but the people had all fled at the approach of the strangers. Spanish priest Bartolomé de las Casas later described the scene: "Several Christians went ashore and walked to some houses that were very artfully made, although of straw and wood; and there was a plaza with a road leading to the sea, very clean and straight, made like a street. . . . Next to the sea was a high watchtower, where ten or twelve people could sit, also well-made. It must have been the pleasure-house of the lord of that island."

Columbus stayed for two days on Borinquén, just long enough to give it a new name. He christened it San Juan Bautista, in honor of Don Juan, the Crown Prince of Spain. This brief visit marks the only time Columbus set foot on land that is now United States territory.

PUERTO RICO

The Spaniards quickly realized that Columbus had not found India after all. Yet the strange new lands that he had discovered by accident might still be a source of wealth and power.

For more than a decade, Spanish ships came and went through the Caribbean, pausing at San Juan Bautista only to take on water and other supplies. Finally, Nicolás de Ovando, the Spanish governor of Santo Domingo on the island of Hispaniola, decided it

A statue of Juan Ponce de León, founder of Puerto Rico's first European settlement, stands outside the Church of San José in San Juan.

was time to see if there was gold on San Juan Bautista. He was also anxious to fortify the island as protection against the Caribs and other enemies. In 1508, the governor sent Juan Ponce de León to establish a village and build a fort.

Ponce de León was not a stranger to the island. He had accompanied Columbus on his voyage in 1493. Now, when he landed his expedition at the Bay of Guánica, a group of Taínos welcomed him. The Indians immediately took him to meet their *cacique*, Agüeybaná.

The Taínos had probably heard from the people of other islands that the pale-skinned newcomers could be treacherous foes. Apparently Agüeybaná decided to win their cooperation with a show of affection. In a great ceremony, he exchanged names with the Spanish leader. According to Taíno belief, the exchange of names would give each man the other's virtues, and bind them in an unbreakable alliance.

Ponce de León set to work at once, searching the island for gold. The Spaniards rejoiced whenever they unearthed a few nuggets of the precious metal, and in triumph, Ponce de León carried some gold samples back to Santo Domingo.

In 1509, he returned to San Juan Bautista to begin mining in earnest. Among the men who came with him was Juan Garrido, a freedman born in West Africa. Garrido was probably the first black person to touch Puerto Rican soil.

Under orders from the king to found a permanent settlement, Ponce de León chose a spot a few miles south of San Juan Bay. There he built a large, sturdy house that could double as a fort and government headquarters. This tiny outpost of Spanish authority was at first called Caparra. In 1521, the settlement moved to a nearby site on a promontory overlooking the Atlantic, and was renamed *Puerto Rico*, meaning "rich port." The name Puerto Rico eventually came to designate the entire island, and the city called Puerto Rico gradually became known as San Juan.

Lying as it did at the entrance to the Caribbean, Puerto Rico was a strategic military outpost. One early Spanish official wrote that the island was "the strongest foothold of Spain in America."

THE QUEST FOR GOLD

The Indians must have been baffled by the strange madness that possessed the Spanish invaders. The newcomers cared for nothing except their ceaseless search for gold. The Indians occasionally used gold for decoration, and the mineral had some religious value for them, but they had never considered it to be very precious.

In 1510, a group of Taínos drowned a Spaniard to find out if Spaniards were mortal.

At first, the Indians were awed by the loud, fire-throwing weapons that the Spaniards had at their command and by the large, thundering beasts they rode upon. Convinced that the strangers were immortal beings, the Indians were too terrified to protest when the Spaniards put them to work as slaves. Then, in 1510, a group of Taínos conducted a daring experiment to see whether the rumors about the white men's immortality were true. As they guided a Spanish settler across a stream, the Indians suddenly shoved him underwater and held him down until he became still. To be certain, they watched over the corpse for three days, until there was no doubt that the man was truly dead.

The news flew across the island, triggering a burst of rebellion. Agüeybaná II, nephew of the *cacique* who had first greeted the Spaniards with such friendliness, led an attack against Ponce himself. In the fighting that followed, Agüeybaná was killed, and the Taínos scattered. Some took to the remote mountains, some

By the 1540s, the slaves on the island were no longer digging and smelting gold, but laboring in the sugarcane fields and sugar mills.

fled to other islands, and some committed suicide to escape further enslavement.

Soon, the Spaniards began using an additional source of slave labor. In 1513, a government edict authorized the use of African slaves in the West Indies. By 1531, more than fifteen hundred black slaves had been brought to Puerto Rico.

Fanning across the island in their search for gold, the Spaniards founded settlements at Guánica, Sotomayor, Daguao, Loíza, and San Germán. But the colony seemed doomed from the start. Hurricanes destroyed crops and swept houses into the sea. Epidemics of smallpox and yellow fever wiped out whole villages. The Caribs and the French plundered towns along the coast. By 1528, the Spaniards had fled from nearly all of their settlements on Puerto Rico. Only San Juan still survived.

To make matters even worse, the supply of gold on the island was running out. Why should the Spaniards endure the rigors of life on Puerto Rico if the island could not even make them rich? Then, early in the 1530s, stories reached Puerto Rico of fabulous discoveries of gold and jewels in the faraway Andes Mountains of South America. Colonists rushed to clamber aboard any departing ship, frantic to reach Peru and steal their share of the treasure.

THE INVINCIBLE OUTPOST

In 1531, a census revealed that only 426 Spaniards lived in Puerto Rico. Gold mining had proved a disappointment. If the colony were ever to prosper, it must develop in a new direction.

The island's tropical climate was ideally suited for growing sugarcane. Sugar was an essential ingredient in the manufacturing of rum, a product that was in constant demand. By the 1540s, the slaves on the island were no longer digging and smelting gold, but laboring in the sugarcane fields under the burning sun.

Yet Spain was interested in Puerto Rico mainly for its strategic military position. Poised at the mouth of the Caribbean, it was perfectly situated to defend the region against invaders. In 1532, construction began on La Fortaleza, a fortress overlooking San Juan Bay. From a military standpoint, however, the site was a poor choice. By the time La Fortaleza was completed in 1540, plans were underway for a second fort at the mouth of the harbor. This second fort, known as El Morro, became the island's chief defense.

Once La Fortaleza and El Morro were in place, San Juan was relatively secure. But the rest of the island remained unprotected. Pirates preyed upon Spanish treasure ships that stopped at the island for supplies. The French and the English, eager to gain control of the Caribbean, launched frequent attacks on outlying settlements. By the end of the 1500s, San Germán had been burned and rebuilt at different sites three times.

In 1588, the famous English sea captain Sir Francis Drake

defeated Spain's prized fleet, the Armada. Fears mounted that Drake would next strike at the Spanish West Indies. Governor Menéndez de Valdés strengthened El Morro, preparing for the inevitable attack.

The assault finally came in 1595. Learning that a vast treasure was stored at La Fortaleza, Drake set out with twenty-seven ships and forty-five hundred men to capture the Spanish gold for Queen Elizabeth of England. Fortunately for the Spaniards, word of the advancing English fleet reached Puerto Rico's governor, Pedro Suárez. Suárez immediately ordered that several Spanish ships be sunk near the entrance to San Juan Bay, thus blocking Drake's fleet as it tried to sail into the harbor.

The English anchored just east of San Juan and attempted to hold the city under siege. But they had not reckoned on the heavy cannons from El Morro and La Fortaleza. One shell hit Drake's cabin while he was at dinner, knocking his stool from under him and killing two of his companions. At last, after several days of heavy bombardment, the English sailed away in defeat.

Three years later, the English once again tried to seize Puerto Rico. George Clifford, third earl of Cumberland, had long coveted the island. He described it as "the very key of the West Indies, which locketh and shuttered all the gold and silver in the continent of America and Brazilia." In June 1598, Cumberland landed his forces on an undefended beach and marched overland toward San Juan. The Puerto Ricans had been severely weakened by a recent epidemic, but they fought fiercely and held off the invaders for several days. At last, however, Cumberland overran the city. On July 1, the English flag was raised over El Morro.

The Puerto Rican people harassed their conquerors mercilessly. Children jeered at the soldiers and pelted them with stones. Women tossed slops at them from balconies. Skirmishes were

In 1595, Sir Francis Drake (above) tried, but failed, to capture La Fortaleza (left).

frequent on the city's narrow streets. Then, the English were stricken with the same epidemic that had earlier devastated the Puerto Ricans.

At last, after occupying San Juan for sixty-five days, Cumberland retreated. He did not leave empty-handed, however. He carried off two thousand slaves, stores of weapons and ammunition, sugar, honey, and spices, and even the bells from the city's churches. When the people of San Juan refused to pay a stiff ransom, Cumberland set the city ablaze and sailed away.

In 1625, Puerto Rico faced a new enemy. Under Bowdoin Hendrick, Dutch forces besieged San Juan, waiting to take the city when food and ammunition ran out. After weeks of fighting, Hendrick wrote to Puerto Rico's governor, threatening to burn San Juan unless he surrendered. "The settlers have enough courage to rebuild their homes," the governor wrote back. "There is timber in the mountains and building material in the land. . . . Do not write any more such letters, for I will not reply.

A seventeenth-century engraving showing a reversed view of San Juan

This is what I choose to answer, and concerning the rest, do as you please."

On October 22, Hendrick set fire to the city. This time, the damage was even greater than it had been at the hands of Cumberland. Perhaps the greatest tragedy was the destruction of a magnificent library that had been brought to the island by Bishop Barnardo de Balbuena. Historians regard Balbuena's library as the finest that existed in the New World at that time.

Early in November, the Dutch finally sailed away from Puerto Rico. Most of San Juan lay in ashes, but the city had again driven away its invaders. As the governor had promised, the people began to rebuild their city once more.

LIFE IN COLONIAL PUERTO RICO

During most of the Spanish colonial period, Puerto Rico operated as a military outpost. The governors appointed by the Spanish Crown were all army or cavalry officers and were given the title of captain general. The governor was responsible not

40

only for the island's defense, but also its economic productivity. Under orders from the king, Puerto Rico's governors encouraged the planting of sugarcane and, later, such crops as ginger, tobacco, and coffee. Yet the governor's budget remained so small that sometimes the island went without the most basic supplies.

The Spanish Crown wanted to squeeze as much revenue as it could from the island. Puerto Rico was forbidden to trade with any other nation except the mother country. This restriction, however, had the reverse effect, for it led to widespread smuggling. People from every social class—farmers, priests, military officers, and many governors—profited from illegal imports and exports. By the middle of the 1700s, Puerto Rico's economy was based on contraband.

Like the military, the Roman Catholic church also wielded tremendous power in the colony. It ran the hospitals and provided the only existing services for the poor. In every town, the church was the focus of social and cultural life.

In 1796, Spain and France joined forces in a war against Great Britain. Eager to destroy Spain's stronghold in the West Indies, the British captured the island of Trinidad early in 1797. On April 17, sixty British ships with nearly ten thousand men anchored off Cangrejos Point east of San Juan. Under General Sir Ralph Abercromby, the British took the present-day town of Santurce and began to bombard San Juan.

By this time, San Juan was not only defended by La Fortaleza and El Morro, but was, like a medieval European city, surrounded by stout stone walls. Governor Don Ramón de Castro gathered militia units from all over the island to defend the capital. After two weeks, the Puerto Ricans once again drove off their would-be invaders. Again Puerto Rico had fought back against a formidable enemy and managed to survive.

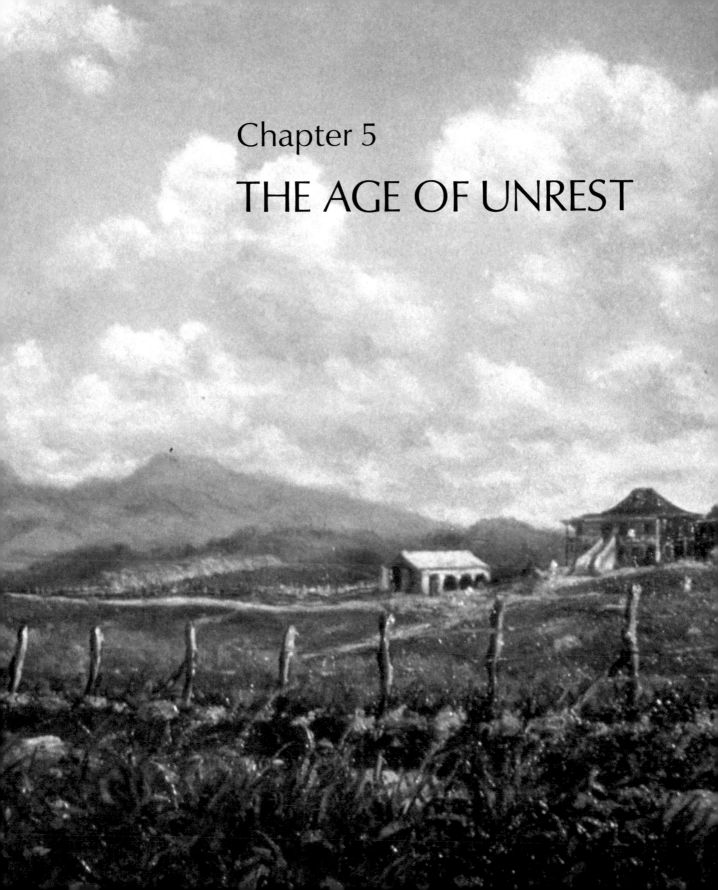

Chapter 5

THE AGE OF UNREST

THE AGE OF UNREST

THE END OF AN EMPIRE

For nearly three hundred years, Spain stood at the helm of a vast empire that had brought it unimaginable wealth and power. Mexico, Central America, Cuba, Santo Domingo, Puerto Rico, most of South America, and the Philippine Islands in the Pacific were all subject to Spanish authority. But gradually, Spain's hold began to weaken. A series of European wars, waged on land and sea, exhausted the motherland's resources. By the close of the eighteenth century, Spain was battered and demoralized, clinging to memories of bygone glory.

In 1808, Napoleon Bonaparte of France invaded Spain and deposed the Spanish king. Although Napoleon's rule was short-lived, Spain's defeat struck the empire a mortal blow. Rebellions flared in Mexico, Venezuela, and elsewhere throughout the colonies.

During the 1810s, thousands of Spanish loyalists from Mexico and South America fled to Puerto Rico. The newcomers were generally wealthier and more conservative than the Puerto Ricans, and were anxious to maintain strong ties with Spain. In Puerto Rico they hoped to live as they had before, as Spaniards simply removed by geography from the mother country.

In an effort to reward the newly arrived Spanish colonists for their loyalty, as well as to appease those Puerto Ricans who might

A diorama of a typical nineteenth-century Puerto Rican sugar plantation

turn rebellious, the Spanish government-in-exile allowed the islanders to send a representative to the *Cortes,* or legislature, in Madrid. Puerto Ricans rejoiced with the appointment of Lieutenant Ramón Power y Giralt to this newly created post. Power set out for Spain with instructions from all of the districts of the island. He was to ask for the establishment of hospitals, public schools, and a university, and for the distribution of land to the poor. Overall, he was charged to work "so that the chains that weigh us down and prevent our development be broken, as demanded by the laws of humanity."

Through Power's efforts, Spain granted Puerto Rico permission to trade with non-Spanish nations and set up a system of free land grants for new settlers. But Spain permitted Puerto Rican representation in the *Cortes* for only a few years. Despite this disappointment, Puerto Rico remained loyal to Spain.

Yet the era of Spanish dominion was over. The empire was crumbling, and colonies all over Spanish America began declaring

In 1849, Governor Juan de Pezuelas passed a repressive law requiring all nonlandowners to carry a *libreta*, or passbook (right), as identification. Anyone caught without a *libreta* had to endure forced labor for eight days.

their independence. By 1824, Spain had only two tiny colonies in the New World—Cuba and Puerto Rico.

THE LITTLE CAESARS

In a desperate attempt to hold onto its last possessions, Spain determined to prevent any further revolutionary activity from flaring up. Instead of rewarding Puerto Rico for its loyalty, the Crown appointed a series of governors who enacted harsher and harsher laws on the island. Beginning in 1822, Puerto Rico was ruled for more than forty years by a series of governor-dictators whom one historian nicknamed the "little Caesars."

Months after he took office, the first of the "little Caesars,"

Miguel de la Torre, forbade all public gatherings after dark and imposed a 10:00 P.M. curfew. But later he decided that people were less likely to stir up trouble if they were having fun. He removed the curfew and vigorously encouraged cockfighting, horseracing, and other entertainment.

Fearing an uprising among the island's slaves, the government passed the *codigo negro*, a series of laws aimed at blacks. A black person who insulted a white was sentenced to five years in prison. Any black who struck a white person was put to death.

In 1849, Governor Juan de Pezuelas required that all agricultural workers on the island carry a *libreta*, or passbook, as identification. Anyone caught without a *libreta* was put to forced labor for eight days. The governor forbade people from traveling between cities, or even having parties without official permission. He shut down the cockpits and racetracks.

Despite the tireless efforts of the governors, however, rebellious rumblings grew louder and louder. The *libreta* law and other repressive measures became hated symbols of Spanish tyranny. Spain's policy toward Puerto Rico did nothing to attack the poverty that lay at the root of the growing discontent.

A handful of wealthy families held nearly all of the cultivated land on the island. They lived in relative luxury, with servants to cook and clean and care for their children. In contrast, thousands of peasants toiled in the sun on the sugar and coffee plantations. Landless farmers, called *jíbaros*, lived as squatters in the remote mountains of the interior. Planting vegetables, gathering wild fruit, and sleeping in woven hammocks inside thatched-roof houses called *bohíos*, the jíbaros survived much as the Taínos had long before them.

In 1855, a devastating epidemic of cholera swept the island. People who seemed healthy in the morning might be writhing in

A family in front of a typical rural dwelling in the 1800s

their death throes when the sun set. By the time the epidemic ran
its course, thirty thousand men, women, and children had died.

All through the heartbreaking months of the sickness,
Dr. Ramón Emeterio Betances worked ceaselessly at the bedsides
of the sick and dying. But his concern for his homeland reached
beyond his work as a physician. Dr. Betances became a leader in
Puerto Rico's ever-strengthening revolutionary movement.

REBELLIONS AND REFORMS

By the late 1850s, Betances, along with Segundo Ruiz Belvis,
Román Baldorioty de Castro, and José Julián Acosta, was one of
the most vocal advocates for change in Puerto Rico's system of
government. He argued for the abolition of slavery and demanded
full civil rights for all Puerto Ricans, rich and poor. In 1862, he
called for Puerto Ricans to take up arms against their Spanish
rulers. At this, the governor ordered him to El Morro and
threatened to hang him for treason. According to legend, Betances

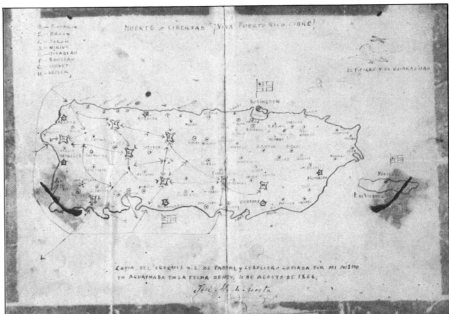

Left: A sculpture of Ramón Emeterio Betances
Above: A draft of the plan for the 1868 uprising
that later became known as *El Grito de Lares*

replied, "The night of that day I shall sleep far more peacefully
than Your Excellency."

After living in exile in St. Thomas and Santo Domingo,
Betances, joined by Belvis, fled to New York. There the two men
joined the *Partido Revolucionario Cubano,* a pro-independence
group made up of Cubans and Puerto Ricans. Returning to Puerto
Rico, Betances founded the Puerto Rican Revolutionary
Committee, which soon had branches all over Puerto Rico. The
committee's password was the letters "l" and "m," which stood
for *Libertad o Muerte,* "liberty or death."

Gradually, the committee made secret plans to go to war. But in
1868, Spanish authorities discovered the plot. Rather than wait to
be arrested, several of the leaders chose to act immediately, ill-
prepared though they were. On the night of September 23,
hundreds of rebels marched into the mountain town of Lares and
captured it with barely a struggle. They declared the existence of a

new nation, the Republic of Puerto Rico, under the provisional presidency of Francisco Ramirez Medina.

Within days, however, the authorities put an end to the uprising. The rebels were routed when they tried to capture the town of San Sebastián. Most fled into the mountains, where Spanish soldiers hunted them down one by one. Today, that event is remembered as *El Grito de Lares*, "The Shout of Lares."

Although Betances failed in his attempt to win Puerto Rican independence, he lived to see one of his cherished hopes fulfilled. In 1873, after more than 350 years, slavery in Puerto Rico was abolished forever. This development was the result of a political upheaval in Spain, in which Queen Isabella II had been overthrown by a powerful group that hoped to make Spain a democracy. The abolition of slavery in Puerto Rico was among the new government's many reforms. In the United States, the practice of slavery ended only after a bloody civil war. In contrast, abolition in Puerto Rico came about quietly and with little fanfare. As a result, some thirty-one thousand slaves were granted their freedom.

Unfortunately, efforts to gain political autonomy for Puerto Rico did not proceed so smoothly. In 1887, Governor Romualdo Palacios González cracked down on all revolutionary talk, writings, and activities. Hundreds of people were arrested, and many of them died under torture. Desperately, the Puerto Ricans pleaded with Spain for an end to this reign of terror, until at last, the governor was removed from office.

More and more Puerto Ricans felt that colonial status was no longer endurable. The Autonomist party, which had formed in the 1880s, began working hard to change Puerto Rico's political status. Luis Muñoz Rivera and other Autonomist party members felt that Puerto Rico should govern itself but maintain strong ties

A scene near Mayagüez in the late 1800s

with Spain. They reasoned that the best way to achieve a measure of self-government would be to fuse with one of Spain's political parties.

In 1895, Muñoz Rivera went to Spain and arranged a pact with Mateo Práxedes Sagasta, the leader of Spain's Liberal party. Sagasta promised that if his party gained control of Spain's government, he would grant Puerto Rico an autonomous government. The Spanish Liberal party came to power in 1897, and Sagasta kept his promise.

That same year, Muñoz Rivera met with the Spanish parliament to design an autonomous form of government for Puerto Rico. Under the new plan, Puerto Rico would still have a governor general appointed by the Spanish Crown. But the island would also have an elected provincial assembly, as well as full representation in the Spanish *Cortes*.

American troops landing at Arroyo in August 1898

The new government went into effect early in July 1898. "Puerto Ricans are generally jubilant," wrote the American consul in San Juan, "and the natives believe that Spain will grant them such a form of home rule as will be in every way satisfactory to them." But the new government had operated for only eight days when gunfire at the town of Guánica altered the course of Puerto Rico's destiny.

THE CONQUEST OF THE UNKNOWN

The United States had long challenged Spain's influence in the Western Hemisphere. In April 1898, hostilities between the two nations flared into war. The United States was determined to capture Spain's last possessions and drive her completely out of the New World.

Because of its strategic location, Puerto Rico was an especially coveted prize. "Do not make peace until we get Puerto Rico,"

A United States regiment marching from Arroyo to Ponce just after the American takeover of the island in 1898

wrote Secretary of the Navy Theodore Roosevelt to his friend Henry Cabot Lodge, as plans for the campaign got underway. "Puerto Rico is not forgotten," Lodge replied, "and we mean to have it."

On May 12, American warships opened fire on the fortifications at San Juan. The assault and the ensuing battle were a comedy of errors. Spain's defensive fire made tremendous noise but missed most of the invading ships. The Americans answered with a barrage of cannonballs that sailed over the walls of the forts and splashed harmlessly into San Juan Bay.

The Americans finally gave up on San Juan, but Puerto Rico was not left in peace for long. On July 25, the USS *Gloucester* landed at Guánica on Puerto Rico's southern coast. American troops disembarked and raised the United States flag above the village. Eleven more warships followed, landing a force of sixteen thousand men under General Nelson A. Miles. "We have not come to make war upon the people of a country that for centuries has been oppressed," Miles announced, "but, on the contrary, to bring you protection, . . . to promote your prosperity, and to bestow upon you the immunities and blessings of the liberal institutions of our government."

Miles met with little resistance as he went on to take the city of Ponce. Few Puerto Ricans had much faith in the new autonomous government, which had been in place for such a short time. They probably suspected that this reform would prove to be as short-lived as so many others had been in the past. Many of the islanders believed that the United States would free them from the hated Spanish colonial rule.

On August 13, Spain signed a treaty with the United States. The terms of the peace agreement required Spain's immediate evacuation from Cuba and Puerto Rico. In a ceremony two months later, the American flag was officially hoisted above La Fortaleza in San Juan. "It was all a quiet affair," Albert Gardner Robinson reported to an American newspaper. "There was no excitement and but little enthusiasm. An hour after the close, the streets had assumed their usual appearance. There was little to show that anything important had taken place, that by this brief ceremony Spain's power on the island of Puerto Rico had ended forever."

Some Puerto Ricans saw the change as a new hope for prosperity on the island. But others, such as Luis Muñoz Rivera, were more cautious. "The island accepted the American invasion with great rejoicing, which I consider premature," Muñoz told the press. "The most elementary discretion counsels a noble and sober reserve until the thinking and action of the Washington legislature is manifested."

In fact, the United States was somewhat at a loss over what to do with the island it had snatched away from Spain. In the past,

American medical officers at Coamo Springs in 1898

new American lands, such as Alaska and the Pacific Northwest, had been largely uninhabited regions, just waiting for settlement. The tiny island of Puerto Rico, in contrast, teemed with nearly a million people. And while the United States was predominantly a nation of Anglo-Saxon Protestants, the Puerto Ricans were staunch Roman Catholics with Indian, African, and Spanish roots. American officials knew almost nothing about the Puerto Rican people—their culture, their politics, their hopes for the future. An American geologist who had worked on the island commented that the United States knew even less about Puerto Rico than it did about Japan and Madagascar.

The United States made a swift and easy conquest in 1898. But it was a conquest whose repercussions would echo through the century to come.

Chapter 6
THE TWENTIETH CENTURY

THE TWENTIETH CENTURY

*This generation that is now beginning must be a
generation with its windows open to all
horizons. . . . The identity of a people is affirmed by
growing with the times rather than by disappearing
with the times.*
—Luis Muñoz Marín, in a speech in Ponce in 1967

A PUPIL OF DEMOCRACY

By 1898, Puerto Rico bore the stamp of more than three
centuries of neglect under Spain. Of the three hundred thousand
school-age children on the island, only some twenty-one
thousand were enrolled in classes. Nearly 80 percent of all Puerto
Ricans were illiterate. Most families lived in crude wooden huts,
many barely surviving on one meal a day. Only 175 miles
(282 kilometers) of paved roads linked the island's towns with
one another. To make matters even worse, 70 percent of the
cultivated land lay in the hands of 2 percent of the people.

To help him formulate his policy toward Puerto Rico, President
William McKinley sent investigators to report on the condition of
the island. A clergyman wrote that the Puerto Rican people were
"moral, industrious, intellectually able, obedient and respectful of
law." However, the military governors placed in temporary
command over Puerto Rico had other ideas. Brigadier General
Guy V. Henry regarded the Puerto Ricans as primitive and
untrustworthy. In 1899, Henry wrote to McKinley, "I understand
that these people are anxious for another form of

government. . . . They are still children. Each one has a different idea, and they don't really know what they want."

The Foraker Act of 1900 reflected the views of Henry and others like him who felt that the Puerto Ricans were not yet ready to govern themselves under the American system. The act created a paternalistic government for the island, run almost entirely by the United States Congress in Washington. Congress controlled the schools, the courts, and the militia. The United States president appointed the island's governor and other key officials. Yet Puerto Ricans were not considered American citizens. The island belonged to, but was not part of, the United States.

Ironically, the Foraker Act was supposed to teach the people of Puerto Rico how to govern themselves. Only after a period of learning about democracy, officials claimed, could Puerto Rico be granted the privileges of home rule.

Despite the drawbacks in the new system, the island made some very real gains in its early years under the United States. Between 1900 and 1910, trade increased nearly 400 percent. New schools were built, and improved sanitation cut down the incidence of disease.

In 1906, Theodore Roosevelt, now president of the United States, paid his first visit to the island he had been so anxious to acquire. He was impressed by the beauty of Puerto Rico's forests and beaches and by the graciousness of its people. "This scheme is working well," he wrote proudly. "No injustice of any kind results from it, and there are great benefits to the island."

PUERTO RICO UNDER THE JONES ACT

Theodore Roosevelt saw Puerto Rico as a land free from injustices. But the thousands of men and women who worked the

In the early 1900s, Luis Muñoz Rivera (above) worked to improve economic conditions in Puerto Rico, where coffee workers (left) earned a mere thirty cents a day.

island's sugar, coffee, and tobacco plantations would have told a different story. Most of the big plantations had been taken over by American companies eager to exploit the island's cheap labor force. Workers in the sugarcane fields earned only fifty-five cents a day. Wages for coffee pickers were a mere thirty cents a day. In 1914, American labor organizer Samuel Gompers visited Arecibo, in the heart of Puerto Rico's sugar country. He deplored the misery of the workers as "a stigma upon the record, the history, and the honor of our country."

Many Puerto Ricans believed that life for the poor would not improve until the island governed itself. In 1916, Luis Muñoz Rivera went before Congress to ask for home rule. Some congressmen argued that Puerto Ricans were not yet well-enough educated to govern themselves. In response, Muñoz pointed out that 80 percent of all Americans were illiterate when the United

A *jíbaro* in front of his palm-leaf house in the mid-1900s

States Constitution had first gone into effect. Nevertheless, Congress voted down the home-rule measure. A few months later, Muñoz died, a deeply disappointed man.

Early in 1917, German submarines torpedoed a Puerto Rican ship off Atlantic City, New Jersey, killing sixteen people. The tragedy sent shock waves across Puerto Rico. The war that had raged in faraway Europe since 1914 now seemed frighteningly close to home.

World War I finally pushed Congress to change the status of Puerto Rico. In March 1917, President Woodrow Wilson signed the Jones Act into law. The Jones Act permitted Puerto Rico to elect its own senate and some of the members of its cabinet. And at last Puerto Ricans were granted American citizenship—just in time to put on khaki uniforms. By the end of the year, eighteen thousand young Puerto Rican men had joined the United States Army.

Although the Jones Act permitted Puerto Ricans more autonomy than they had known before, Washington still gripped the reins. The United States president selected the island's governor, supreme court justices, and many cabinet members. Furthermore, Congress had the right to amend the Jones Act at any time, without Puerto Rico's consent.

The shortcomings of the Jones Act soon became painfully clear. In 1921, President Warren Harding appointed one of his political cronies, E. Montgomery Reilly, to serve as the island's governor. Reilly was a businessman who knew almost nothing about Puerto Rico, but he enjoyed giving orders and expected to be obeyed. In his inaugural address, Reilly declared, "My friends, there is no room on this island for any flag other than the Stars and Stripes. So long as Old Glory waves over us, it will continue to wave over Puerto Rico."

THE RISE OF NATIONALISM

Governor Reilly's attitude toward Puerto Rican independence left an enduring legacy—an ever-more vocal nationalist movement. Many Puerto Ricans had hoped to gain self-government by working with the United States through legal channels. Now nationalists began to feel that the United States would respond only to force.

In 1928, a hurricane, called San Felipe because it occurred on the feast day of St. Philip, killed three hundred people and destroyed a quarter of a million homes. Half of the coffee crop and one-third of the sugarcane crop were left in ruins.

San Felipe gave the last push to an economy that already teetered on the brink of collapse. Sugar and coffee prices had tumbled since World War I. While unemployment climbed, the

In 1937, in what is remembered as the Ponce Massacre, police and marchers exchanged gunfire during a nationalist demonstration in Ponce.

population was also rising steadily by some forty thousand people per year. All of the best cropland on the island belonged to a handful of individuals and private corporations. By 1929, one journalist described Puerto Rico as "a land of beggars and millionaires."

During the 1930s, the world reeled under history's most devastating economic depression. The plight of Puerto Rico seemed almost hopeless. Programs under President Franklin Roosevelt's "New Deal" established free health clinics and encouraged rural people to grow their own food in home truck gardens. But the New Deal scarcely touched the problems of thousands of unemployed coffee and cane workers.

By 1937, Puerto Rican nationalists, led by Pedro Albizu Campos, were calling for armed revolution. In March, a group of

Luis Muñoz Marín, shown here talking with a group of *jíbaros*, founded the Popular Democratic party, whose emblem (above) symbolized its commitment to agrarian reform.

Puerto Rican nationalists asked to hold a parade in Ponce. When the governor refused to issue a permit, the marchers gathered anyway. To this day, no one knows where the first shot came from, but in answer, the police fired into the crowd. When the ensuing riot was over, twenty-one people lay dead. History remembers this tragic episode as the Ponce Massacre.

Like his father, Luis Muñoz Rivera, Luis Muñoz Marín was passionately dedicated to the cause of Puerto Rican autonomy. But unlike the more radical nationalists, he favored peaceful means to bring about change. In 1938, Muñoz Marín founded the *Partido Popular Democrático* (Popular Democratic Party [PDP]). Clearly identifying itself with Puerto Rico's hardworking rural population, the PDP chose as its emblem the profile of a *jíbaro* wearing a typical straw hat. The party's slogan was *Pan, Tierra, y Libertad*, "Bread, Land, and Liberty." The PDP captured four

63

An all-Puerto Rican army unit poses while off-duty in Manila during World War II.

districts on the island in the local elections of 1940. But once
again, it took a war to make the United States reevaluate its
relationship with Puerto Rico.

PUERTO RICO BECOMES A COMMONWEALTH

Some sixty-five thousand Puerto Ricans served in the armed
forces during World War II. The Puerto Rican troops of the Sixty-
fifth Infantry fought in North Africa, and later crossed the Alps to
sweep into Germany.

Throughout the war years, Puerto Rico played a major role in
the defense of the Caribbean region. President Roosevelt grew
increasingly concerned about the island's loyalty to the United

This 1941 photograph shows newly appointed governor Rexford Guy Tugwell (left) shaking hands with his predecessor, Guy Swope (right). Luis Muñoz Marín, then president of the Puerto Rican Senate, stands between them.

States. In 1941 he appointed Rexford Guy Tugwell to govern Puerto Rico.

Most of the federally appointed governors who preceded Tugwell knew little about Puerto Rico. Few even bothered to learn Spanish. Tugwell, however, had studied the island's culture and history, and was determined to do everything in his power to improve conditions. Working closely with Muñoz Marín and other Puerto Rican leaders, he brought running water and electricity to remote mountain villages and distributed more than 15,000 acres (6,070 hectares) of land as homesteads for poor farmers. In 1943, he warned a Senate subcommittee, "American policy in Puerto Rico has the choice of economic assistance with a rather hopeful prospect, or of suppressing an angry people who would feel very deeply that they had been wronged. . . . Two million people cannot permanently be kept in the twilight of colonialism."

Tugwell's attitude toward the island ushered in a new era in United States-Puerto Rico relations. In 1947, Congress amended the Jones Act with the Butler-Crawford Bill. The new bill allowed Puerto Ricans to elect their own governor, who could in turn appoint cabinet officials.

For the first time in more than four hundred years, Puerto Ricans went to the polls and voted for a governor. Overwhelmingly, they chose longtime activist Luis Muñoz Marín.

Yet even greater changes were afoot. On July 3, 1950, President Harry Truman signed Public Law 600, known as the Constitution Act. The Constitution Act granted Puerto Rico status as a United States commonwealth. While still maintaining close ties with the United States, Puerto Ricans would have the right to design their own government based on their own constitution.

Muñoz Marín and his supporters rejoiced over the Constitution Act. But some Puerto Ricans thought that it did not go far enough. Those who wanted Puerto Rico to become a full-fledged state felt that the island was being pushed aside by an uncaring federal government. Puerto Rican nationalists, on the other hand, resented the ongoing connection with the United States. Advocates of Puerto Rican independence described commonwealth status as "perfumed colonialism."

Militant nationalist leader Pedro Albizu Campos prepared for an armed revolution. In October 1950, he spearheaded the takeover of two inland towns, Jayuya and Utuado. Another band of nationalists attacked the governor's palace. By the time the militia put down the uprising, thirty-three people had been killed.

After nine months of discussion and debate, Puerto Rico's constitutional convention drew up a body of laws for the commonwealth. The constitution reflected Puerto Rico's commitment to the democratic process and to the advancement of

A national guardsman escorts captured nationalists to a prisoner compound
after the attempted nationalist takeover of Jayuya in October 1950.

human rights. It also made it clear that Puerto Rico would
maintain a permanent association with the United States. Puerto
Ricans retained their United States citizenship, yet were not
required to pay federal income tax. They could vote for
government officials on the island, though they could not vote for
the United States president and had no voting representatives in
Congress. The island would continue to use American currency,
as it had since 1899. Yet, like any sovereign nation, Puerto Rico
was now entitled to its own flag and national anthem.

On July 25, 1952, Governor Muñoz Marín raised the Puerto
Rican flag beside the Stars and Stripes over El Morro. The date for
the ceremony had been carefully chosen. It was on July 25, 1898,
that Nelson Miles had landed at Guánica. Exactly fifty-four years
later, Puerto Rico was no longer a colony, but an autonomous
commonwealth of the United States.

On July 25, 1952, the day Puerto Rico was proclaimed a commonwealth, Governor Muñoz Marín raised the Puerto Rican flag alongside the Stars and Stripes at El Morro.

The commonwealth arrangement outraged the most passionate Puerto Rican nationalists. On March 1, 1954, three men and a woman entered the visitors' gallery of the United States House of Representatives and opened fire, shouting, "Puerto Rico is not free!" Five congressmen were wounded, and the assailants were arrested and sentenced to life imprisonment. But the attack on Congress had little impact on relations between Puerto Rico and the United States.

QUESTIONS AND CHALLENGES

Since the passage of the Jones Act in 1917, there had been a steady trickle of Puerto Ricans into the United States. During the 1950s, the trickle suddenly became a vast flood. Tens of thousands of people from Puerto Rico formed large Spanish-speaking communities in New York and other industrial northeastern cities. Like other immigrant groups before them, many took low-paying factory jobs and fought their way up the social ladder.

Yet the inner city could be cruel. Schools were underequipped and poorly staffed; crumbling tenements and housing projects were infested with rats. Too often, young people became ensnared by illegal drugs and gang warfare. In the concrete jungles of Manhattan and Newark, Puerto Ricans sometimes yearned for the lush green island they had left behind.

For those who remained in Puerto Rico, the 1950s and 1960s brought enormous changes. Sugar and coffee no longer ruled supreme. Under Muñoz Marín, a series of government programs called Operation Bootstrap forged a new industrial economy. American companies invested in plants that manufactured such products as clothing, electrical equipment, and chemicals. The factories created thousands of new jobs, luring families from the countryside to the cities.

But Muñoz's goals reached far beyond economic development. He worked to build an ideal society that would never lose respect for human decency, one in which education, health care, and adequate housing would be available for everyone. By the early 1960s, Puerto Rico served as a model for the struggling nations of Latin America.

The 1970s brought inflation and economic recession to Puerto Rico. As jobs dried up and the cost of living climbed, more and more islanders had to depend upon food stamps and other federal programs to meet their basic needs. The standard of living in Puerto Rico remained well below that of the United States. However, Puerto Ricans still enjoyed far greater prosperity than the people of most Caribbean and Latin American countries.

THE QUEST FOR IDENTITY

Every year, on the morning of July 25, a parade in San Juan celebrates the day when Puerto Rico became a United States commonwealth. In the afternoon on that day, demonstrators march in Guánica to decry the United States invasion in 1898, and to protest the continued political connection between the island and the United States.

Puerto Rico has its own history and culture, a heritage of which its people are justly proud. Yet Puerto Rico's relationship with the United States is a source of endless conflict. Throughout the 1980s, debate raged over the island's status—whether it should remain a commonwealth, seek independence, or become the fifty-first state of the Union.

One of the strongest advocates of statehood is former governor Carlos Romero Barceló, leader of the New Progressive party. "The United States is the only nation in the hemisphere with a colony," he argues. "It's a smear on its face and a shame on Puerto Rico." On the other hand, Carlos M. Ayes, an eloquent nationalist, contends that "statehood will mean war. If the United States wants its very own Northern Ireland, let them continue this farce."

In 1990, a study by the Congressional Budget Office concluded that a change in Puerto Rico's status would be disastrous to the island's economy. If Puerto Rico became a state, individuals and corporations would have to pay federal income tax for the first time. The loss of tax incentives might persuade many companies to cut back their investments in the island. "As a result of this report, key congressional committees will no longer in good conscience include statehood or independence as realistic alternatives," said Jaime B. Fuster, Puerto Rico's nonvoting

Governor Carlos Romero Barceló (with flag) joined in the festivities at the annual Puerto Rican Day Parade in New York in 1977.

delegate to Congress. "There is no way that Congress is going to offer the Puerto Rico voters an option that . . . causes 100,000 jobs to be lost."

As it sorts out its relationship with the United States, Puerto Rico will find ways to preserve and enhance its unique identity. "Although Puerto Ricans may learn English and be influenced by many American ways, the basic ties cannot be a common language or common historical and ethnic tradition," states historian Arturo Morales Carrión. "The ties have to be found elsewhere, in the common belief in and loyalty to democratic values, or in the common hope that there are meeting grounds for understanding, mutual interest and respect beyond the frontiers of absorbing nationalism."

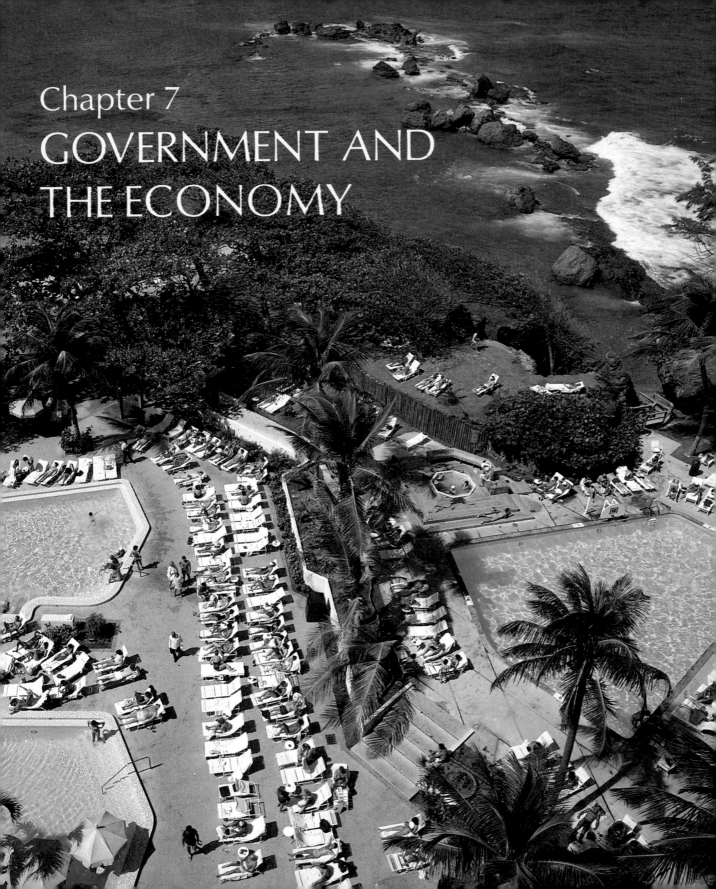

Chapter 7
GOVERNMENT AND
THE ECONOMY

GOVERNMENT AND THE ECONOMY

As a commonwealth of the United States, Puerto Rico is governed by its own constitution, ratified in 1952. In many ways, Puerto Rico is like one of the fifty states. It uses American currency and is subject to federal laws that govern communication and interstate commerce. Yet Puerto Ricans do not have all the rights of other American citizens. They cannot vote in presidential elections. They elect a resident commissioner to Congress, who has a voice on committees, but cannot vote on legislation.

Modeled on the United States federal government, the government of Puerto Rico is divided into three branches. The legislative branch passes and repeals laws; the judicial branch, or court system, interprets the laws; and the executive branch, or office of the governor, ensures that the laws are carried out.

The governor, elected by Puerto Rico's voters, may serve an unlimited number of four-year terms. If the governor should die in office or resign before completing the term, he or she is succeeded by the secretary of state. With the approval of the legislature, the governor appoints the heads of many government departments, as well as justices to serve on the supreme court.

The supreme court at San Juan is the highest court on the island. It has a chief justice and seven associate justices, who may serve until they reach the age of seventy. Below the supreme court is the superior court, the major trial court in the commonwealth. District courts and municipal courts hear cases on the local level.

Puerto Rico's legislative assembly is composed of a senate and a house of representatives. The number of senators and representatives varies from election to election. Some of these legislators are elected by district, and others are chosen at large by all of the voters on the island. Regular sessions of the legislature begin on the second Monday in January and last until all business has been completed. In times of emergency, the governor may call a special legislative session.

Puerto Rico is not divided into counties, as are each of the fifty states. Instead, local government is conducted through the island's seventy-eight *municipios*, or municipalities. Some *municipios* are cities, while others center around tiny villages and include many scattered rural homesteads. Each municipality elects a mayor and municipal assembly to make local laws.

EDUCATION

Since 1898, education has been a priority in Puerto Rico. When Nelson Miles landed at Guánica, only 23 percent of Puerto Ricans could read and write. By 1980, the literacy rate had risen to 90 percent. Today, about 693,000 students attend public schools on the island, and another 118,000 are enrolled in parochial schools.

Founded in 1903, the University of Puerto Rico is the largest institution of higher learning in the commonwealth. The main campus of the university is at Río Piedras, but there are also branches in Mayagüez, San Juan, Cayey, and Humacao. The university's schools of dentistry and tropical medicine are located in Old San Juan, and the college of agriculture is based in Mayagüez.

In addition to the University of Puerto Rico, the commonwealth has more than thirty other public and private colleges and universities. Among them are Inter American University of Puerto

The University of Puerto Rico is the island's largest institution of higher learning.

Rico, with campuses in Hato Rey and San Germán; Catholic University of Puerto Rico at Ponce; and the University of the Sacred Heart in Santurce.

TRANSPORTATION AND COMMUNICATION

Trucks and cars in Puerto Rico roll over more than 7,000 miles (11,265 kilometers) of paved roads and highways. In the Cordillera Central, some of the older, twisting, narrow roads offer the visitor breathtaking views and an occasional moment of heart-stopping terror. Puerto Rico International Airport in San Juan is the island's major airfield. San Juan is also one of the chief seaports in the Caribbean. The port of Mayagüez has a unique duty-free trade zone.

About one-third of Puerto Rico's cropland is planted in sugarcane.

Puerto Rico's first newspaper, *La Gaceta de Puerto Rico*, appeared in 1807. Today, all of the commonwealth's major papers are published in San Juan. These include *El Nuevo Día* and *El Vocero*. The *San Juan Star* is the island's major English-language daily.

Radio and television stations in Puerto Rico broadcast in both Spanish and English. Radio came to the island in 1922, when WKAQ went on the air in San Juan. The island's first television station, WKAQ-TV, began broadcasting in 1954. Today Puerto Ricans can choose among nearly a hundred AM and FM radio stations and about ten television stations.

AGRICULTURE

For four centuries, agriculture, especially cattle raising, was the backbone of Puerto Rico's economy. Today, however, farming accounts for only 2 percent of the gross domestic product—the

Coffee, grown mainly in the western part of the Cordillera Central, is Puerto Rico's second-most-important crop.

total value of all goods and services produced on the island within a given year.

About 60 percent of Puerto Rico's land is under cultivation. Half of Puerto Rico's twenty-nine thousand farms are very tiny— 10 acres (4 hectares) or less in size. Farmers working these small plots raise food for themselves and their families, with little left over to take to market. Some two thousand large farms account for about 80 percent of the agricultural products exported by Puerto Rico.

Sugarcane is Puerto Rico's leading crop, as it was in the eighteenth century. About one of every five farm workers on the island are engaged in the sugarcane industry. Sugarcane grows chiefly on the lowlands along the coast. Coffee, the island's leading crop in the nineteenth century, is today Puerto Rico's second-most-important export crop. Most Puerto Rican tobacco is

Pineapples are among a number of tropical fruits harvested in Puerto Rico.

used in the manufacture of cigars. Other crops raised on the island include bananas, pineapples, plantains, coconuts, and citrus fruits.

Milk and cheese head the list of Puerto Rico's livestock products. Poultry is also important; chicken is a staple in Puerto Rican cuisine.

MANUFACTURING

After World War II, Puerto Rico shifted from an agricultural economy to one based on manufacturing. Today, manufacturing accounts for 39 percent of the gross domestic product. Some 2,300 factories employ about 140,000 workers on the island.

The clothing industry developed during the 1930s, when companies employed groups of seamstresses to work at sewing machines in small shops. By the 1980s, more people worked in clothing manufacture than in any other single industry in the commonwealth. Other manufactured products include chemicals,

A cruise ship in San Juan Harbor

including medicines; food products, including refined sugar; electrical equipment; and scientific instruments.

SERVICE INDUSTRIES

Every year, about 2 million tourists visit Puerto Rico. They bask on its beaches, watch its colorful festivals, dine on seafood, and relax at luxury hotels. Tourism is only one aspect of Puerto Rico's service industries—industries that produce services for individuals or groups.

Altogether, service industries account for about 57 percent of Puerto Rico's gross domestic product. Wholesale and retail trade are among the most important service industries in the commonwealth. Finance, insurance, and real-estate industries are centered in and around San Juan. Tourism, though centered in the San Juan area, is developing throughout the island.

PUERTO RICAN CULTURE

LITERATURE

During its first three centuries as a Spanish colony, Puerto Rico had little chance to develop a body of literature. Few books were available, and there was no printing press on the island. Only a handful of people could read and write. The earliest account of life on the island appeared in 1582, in *Memorial and General Description of the Island of Puerto Rico* by Juan García Troche and Antonio de Santa Clara. A priest named Fray Iñigo Abad y Lasierra published his comprehensive *Geographical, Civil and Political History of the Island of San Juan Bautista de Puerto Rico* in 1788. This work is not only an important source on Puerto Rican history, but is also rich in folklore and descriptions of village life.

In 1807, the first printing press was finally brought to the island, ushering in a new era in the publication of books and periodicals. Despite repression by the Spaniards, who feared that writers would try to spark a revolution, Puerto Rican literature flowered in the nineteenth century.

Published in 1849, *El gíbaro*, by Manuel A. Alonso, depicts rural life in Puerto Rico as a rollicking series of weddings, festivals, and cockfights. But Eugenio María de Hostos, one of the leading intellectuals of nineteenth-century Latin America, revealed the grimmer side of life on the island. Thinly disguised as fiction, his *Pilgrimage of Bayoán* exposes the harshness of Spanish colonial rule. Hostos's richly varied works include collections of nursery rhymes, a national hymn to Puerto Rico, and even a humorous essay on Shakespeare's *Hamlet*.

In his novel *La charca (The Pond)*, published in 1894, Manuel Zeno Gandía set a new tone of realism for Puerto Rican writers. The novel contrasts the natural beauty of the island with the bitter hardships of workers on a large coffee plantation.

Other important Puerto Rican writers of the 1800s include romantic poets José Gautier Benítez and Lola Rodríguez de Tío, and prose writers Alejandro Tapia y Rivera and Salvador Brau.

Virgilio Davila's 1917 book *Pueblito de antes* (*Little Town of Long Ago*) is sometimes compared to Thornton Wilder's classic play *Our Town*. With a nostalgic romanticism, Davila re-creates the ordinary joys and sorrows of the people in a close-knit Puerto Rican village.

One of Puerto Rico's most revered poets is Luis Lloréns Torres, whose works were brought together in the 1940 collection *Alturas de America* (*Heights of America*). In poems such as "La Canción de las Antillas" ("Song of the Antilles"), Lloréns celebrates the heritage of the Caribbean.

René Marqués is best known for his plays and short stories, but his novel *La víspera del hombre* (*The Sundown of Man*) won a Faulkner Foundation Prize in 1962. His play *Juan bobo y la dama del Occidente* (*Foolish Juan and the Lady from the West*) parodies the traditional Puerto Rican motif of happy rural life. *La carreta* (*The Cart*) is a drama about a family that leaves its mountain village for New York City, only to find tragedy and disillusionment.

As more and more young Puerto Ricans migrated to the United States, this theme of dislocation became central to Puerto Rican literature. Probably the best-known emigré writer is Piri Thomas, whose autobiography, *Down These Mean Streets*, offers shocking descriptions of life in New York's Spanish Harlem.

Portraits by José Campeche

In the 1970s and 1980s, many gifted young Puerto Rican writers began to win recognition. Luis Rafael Sánchez began his career as a playwright, but is best-known for his novel *Macho Camacho's Beat*. In her short stories and her novel *Buenos días, Tío Sergio* (*Hello, Uncle Sergio*), Magali García Ramis explores middle-class values and questions the traditional role of women in society.

ART

Puerto Rico's first painter of note was José Campeche, born in 1752 in San Juan. Campeche was almost entirely self-taught, and made his own paints from the juices of plants and flowers. Most of his works, painted on copper or wood rather than on canvas, depict saints or Madonnas. His *British Siege* commemorates the defense of San Juan in 1797.

Francisco Oller, a native of Bayamón, became famous for his

El velorio, by Francisco Oller

landscapes, portraits, and lively regional scenes. Oller studied in Spain and France, and knew such great nineteenth-century painters as Paul Cézanne and Édouard Manet. One of his best-known works is *El velorio* (*The Wake*), a panoramic scene depicting villagers carrying on during a wake for a small child. The generation that followed Oller included such talented artists as Impressionist Ramón Frade.

Enthusiasm for the graphic arts dawned in Puerto Rico in the 1950s and 1960s. The etchings of Antonio Martorell have earned international acclaim. Every two years, the Institute of Puerto Rican Culture in San Juan hosts an exhibition of graphic arts, bringing in work from all over Latin America and the Caribbean.

The late twentieth century witnessed a revival of interest in Puerto Rican folk art. Young artists carried on the ancient tradition of carving detailed images of saints from wood. Some carvers have turned their skills to creating vivid sculptures representing scenes in daily life. Other artists make pottery, weave

Above: A mask made by a Ponce artisan for use during *Carnival*
Right: Puerto Rican instruments, including (from left) a *cuatro*, *maracas*, a *tiple*, and a *güiro*

rugs, and do fine embroidery, bringing fresh life to centuries-old island traditions. Artisans in Ponce and Loíza are famous for their wild, colorful masks.

MUSIC

Without a doubt, music is Puerto Rico's richest form of artistic expression. The Taínos danced and feasted to the accompaniment of gourd rattles called *maracas* as well as the *güiro*, a long, hollow gourd played with a stick. These and other ancient instruments, now made of wood or plastic, are still used in popular music on the island. Recent years have seen a revival of interest in other traditional instruments. These include the *cuatro*, a guitarlike instrument with five pairs of strings; and the *tiple*, which resembles the ukelele.

The harmonies of Spanish church music and the rhythms and power of African dances also have made an essential contribution to Puerto Rico's musical heritage. The African influence on Puerto Rican music is clearly seen in the *plena*, a highly rhythmic dance accompanied by a wide variety of hand-held percussion instruments. The form of music known as the *danza* was first enjoyed by upper-class Puerto Ricans in the 1800s. Today, usually played by a string and woodwind orchestra, the *danza* opens with a sedate, dignified section, then breaks into a wildly exuberant dance tune. During the 1890s, Juan Morel Campos perfected the *danza* with such outstanding compositions as "Laura y Georgina" and "No me toques" ("Don't Touch Me").

During the twentieth century, music has been an eloquent vehicle for nationalistic feeling in Puerto Rico. Immensely popular singer and composer Rafael Hernández wrote love laments and humorous lyrics, but he is best remembered for songs that stir Puerto Rican pride. In "Preciosa" ("Precious"), one of his most beloved pieces, he sings of an island without glory, mistreated by tyrants, but precious to its people all the same.

A new brand of popular dance music emerged in Cuba and Puerto Rico in the late 1900s. Because of its spiciness or "soul," this music was called *salsa*, meaning "sauce." Salsa is a zesty blend of Latin and Afro-Caribbean music with the "Big Band" sound of American jazz. Tito Puente, one of salsa's originators, describes it as "all our fast Latin music put together." Salsa groups generally include a piano and bass, horn and percussion sections, and a chorus and lead vocalist.

Internationally renowned cellist Pablo Casals gave a boost to the popularity of classical music in Puerto Rico when he settled on the island, his mother's homeland, in 1956. Casals established the Puerto Rico Conservatory of Music, and founded and directed

A display of deep-fried Puerto Rican specialties at a sidewalk cafe

the Puerto Rico Symphony Orchestra. The Pablo Casals Music Festival, held each June in San Juan, draws performers and music lovers from all over the world.

CUISINE

Puerto Rican cuisine makes excellent use of a wide variety of ingredients—some of them native to the island, others imported since the coming of the Spaniards. The versatile plantain or *plátano*, which resembles a large, green banana, can be roasted, boiled, or baked. Sliced and deep-fried, it is served as a crispy side dish much like french-fried potatoes. Plantain leaves are used to wrap *pasteles*, tamales made of a paste of mashed plantain and *yautía* (a starchy tuber) and stuffed with meat and raisins.

Since Puerto Rico is an island, it is not surprising that many delicious recipes are based on seafood. Shrimp, squid, codfish, or lobster are mixed with rice and black beans in a rich stew called *asopao*. Pork and poultry dishes are also popular. The flavor of olive oil, used in frying and sautéing, enhances most meals. Puerto Rican cooks are masters in the use of fresh ginger, oregano, and cilantro.

The stalls in a Puerto Rican market overflow with a dazzling array of tropical fruits. Oranges, lemons, melons, and pineapples are familiar to visitors from the United States mainland. But such tropical fruits as the sweet, yellowish *jobo*, the spiny, dark-green *guanabana*, and the starchy breadfruit are new to most northerners. The star apple reveals a delicate star pattern when it is cut in half.

SPORTS

Baseball is Puerto Rico's national sport. In Puerto Rico, the baseball season runs from October through January. The island has its own baseball leagues, with stadiums in every major city. Puerto Rico has given the major leagues many outstanding players. An all-star team made up of Puerto Ricans might include hard-hitting Orlando Cepeda, born in Ponce, at first base. The infield could be rounded out by Felix Millán of Yabucoa and José Pagán, born in Barceloneta. Speedy José Cruz of Arroyo might play the outfield, along with the great Roberto Clemente.

Roberto Clemente, a native of Carolina, is Puerto Rico's most cherished baseball hero. Few other players possessed his all-around excellence in hitting, running, and throwing. In addition, he brought an unmatched competitive fire to the field. Playing for the Pittsburgh Pirates, Clemente ran the bases with relentless fury and boldly dived after every fly ball that came near his position of right field. He lived and died a humanitarian. Clemente was killed in 1972 in an airplane crash near Puerto Rico while flying emergency food and medical supplies to earthquake victims in Nicaragua.

Basketball is also a popular team sport. Puerto Rican teams compete against teams from throughout Latin America and the Caribbean. Puerto Rican athletes also compete in boxing, weightlifting, and swimming. Puerto Rico sends its own team to the Olympic Games.

Cockfighting has long been a popular sport in Puerto Rico, and cockpits draw crowds in every city and town. As the roosters fight to the death, the people in the stands bet wildly on which will survive. The most popular racetrack on the island is San Juan's El Comandante, which opened in 1956.

Deep-sea fishermen set out from Puerto Rico every day in the hope of catching marlin, mackerel, barracuda, and red snapper. Divers in scuba gear delight in the underwater world of sculpted coral and darting, jewel-like fishes. During the winter months, surfers from around the world challenge the waves off Rincón's beaches.

FESTIVALS

Every year on the evening of June 23, crowds gather along the beaches at San Juan. At the stroke of midnight, young and old, even the mayor of the city, walk backward into the waves. This ceremony is part of San Juan's traditional celebration of the feast day of its patron saint, John the Baptist. Walking backward into the water is said to assure good luck through the coming year.

Each town in Puerto Rico has a patron saint whose feast day in the Roman Catholic calendar becomes a local festival. Ferris

wheels and games of chance are set up in the plaza. The music, dancing, food, and gambling last for a week.

Some religious holidays, on the other hand, are very solemn occasions. In the town of Hormigueros, the devout honor the feast day of Our Lady of the Monsarrat by climbing the steep stone steps to the church on their knees. Throughout the island, Good Friday is a day for solemn processions and Masses.

In addition to its religious festivals, Puerto Rico celebrates many holidays not observed on the United States mainland. January 11 commemorates the birthday of Puerto Rican writer and educator Eugenio María de Hostos. March 22 marks the date when, in 1873, slavery was abolished on the island. On April 16, Puerto Ricans remember the birthday of patriot José de Diego. The birthday of another patriotic leader, Luis Muñoz Rivera, is celebrated on July 17. July 25 is the anniversary of both the day in 1952 when Puerto Rico became a commonwealth, and the American invasion of Puerto Rico in 1898. On July 27, Puerto Rico honors the birthday of José Celso Barbosa, a dedicated advocate of statehood in the early 1900s. November 19, Discovery Day, recalls the day when Columbus landed on the island in 1493.

Chapter 9
A VISIT TO THE ISLAND OF ENCHANTMENT

A VISIT TO THE ISLAND OF ENCHANTMENT

Most foreign visitors to Puerto Rico are lured by its glistening beaches and luxury hotels. But travelers with a bit of curiosity will quickly discover that the island has many other attractions as well. Surprises lurk around every corner in colonial Old San Juan. Colorful festivals bring sleepy mountain villages gloriously to life. Tropical birds and flowers thrive in fourteen forest areas under the Puerto Rico Department of Natural Resources. It is no wonder that Puerto Rico has earned the nickname *Isla del Encanto*, "Island of Enchantment."

SAN JUAN

With nearly one-third of Puerto Rico's population, San Juan is the cultural, political, and economic hub of the island. The oldest portion of the city is an area of seven square blocks perched on a peninsula overlooking the Atlantic. Old San Juan has been designated a historic landmark, and many of its houses, churches, and shops have been restored to look as they did in the seventeenth and eighteenth centuries. It is said that the bluish bricks that pave the streets were originally used as ballast on the early Spanish ships. Though this may be pure legend, there is no doubt that parts of the original walls that once surrounded Old San Juan are still intact.

Three massive fortresses guarded San Juan under the Spanish governors, and all still stand today. The Fort of San Felipe del Morro (known as El Morro) is a masterpiece of military

The famous fortress known as El Morro lies at the entrance of San Juan Bay.

engineering. Its walls, 20 feet (6 meters) thick in places, were almost immune to cannonfire. A network of ramps and stairways was designed for the swift movement of artillery and troops in an emergency.

Enclosing some 27 acres (11 hectares) of grounds, San Cristobal is the largest of San Juan's fortifications and was the biggest in the Spanish Empire. The fort is divided into five units that could be closed off from one another and defended separately if part of the fort were taken by enemies.

La Fortaleza, San Juan's third fort, serves as the governor's mansion. It is the oldest executive residence in the Western Hemisphere. Among La Fortaleza's many fascinating rooms are the Chamber of Mirrors, the restored old kitchen in the south tower, and the John F. Kennedy room, a guest room for visiting

Boys peeking over a wall at El Morro

dignitaries. In a gallery off the main courtyard stands an antique grandfather clock. According to an old story, the governor of Puerto Rico struck the clock with the flat of his sword when he was told he must yield to the invading Americans in 1898. The hands of the clock are fixed at 4:30, marking forever that fateful moment in history.

Dating back to 1523, the Dominican Convent is one of the earliest buildings in Old San Juan. Today it houses the Institute of Puerto Rican Culture, a highly diverse and influential organization that encourages the arts on the island. Galleries around the central courtyard display the work of contemporary

San Juan's historic Customs House (left) and Provincial Deputation Building (right)

Puerto Rican artists. The institute oversees the restoration of historic buildings in Old San Juan and throughout the island.

Most of the original Cathedral of San Juan has been destroyed or covered by newer parts of the building. The present structure was completed in the nineteenth century. Buried here are the remains of Juan Ponce de León, who came to Puerto Rico with Columbus in 1493 and served as the island's first Spanish governor.

Another attraction of Old San Juan is the Buttress House, a magnificent eighteenth-century mansion. It houses the Pharmacy Museum, a collection of jars, measures, and other memorabilia from a nineteenth-century drugstore. Also within the Buttress House are the Center for Taíno Crafts and the Latin American Engravings Museum. Just around the corner is the Pablo Casals

An aerial view of Condado, San Juan

Museum, dedicated to the memory of the renowned cellist who made Puerto Rico his home for twenty years. The museum houses a collection of Casals's letters and other papers, a library of tapes made at the Casals Festivals, and, in a place of honor, the master's cello.

The Condado district is the commercial center of San Juan. Elegant hotels line beaches crowded with sunbathing tourists. Away from the sea stand stores and office buildings. In sharp contrast to Old San Juan, Condado is a modern landscape of glass and steel.

Puerto Rico's capitol is located in the section of San Juan known as Puerta de Tierra. Inside the capitol dome are four murals, depicting Columbus's discovery of Puerto Rico, Spanish

Puerto Rico's capitol lies in
the section of San Juan
known as Puerta de Tierra.

colonization, the early independence movement, and the abolition
of slavery. At the center of the rotunda stands an urn that
contains Puerto Rico's original constitution, ratified in 1952.

Just south of San Juan, Río Piedras is the home of the main
campus of the University of Puerto Rico. One of the university's
major landmarks is the Franklin D. Roosevelt Tower, built in the
late 1930s. The university maintains a fine archaeological museum
with artifacts of early Caribbean civilizations. Visitors to Río
Piedras delight in the Botanical Gardens, which display some two
hundred species of tropical plants and trees. A maze of paths leads
to the Lotus Lagoon, the Orchid Garden, and the Bamboo
Promenade.

Bayamón, considered part of the San Juan metropolitan area, is
sometimes called "Puerto Rico's most progressive city." It seems

Arecibo is an industrial city located on the northern coast west of San Juan.

that there are always new highways, office buildings, and apartment complexes under construction. Bayamón's population has mushroomed in recent decades, making it the second-largest city on the island.

WESTERN PUERTO RICO

The roads along the Atlantic coast pass dense fields of sugarcane, a reminder of the role sugar played in Puerto Rico's early history. Sugar refineries and rum distilleries employ thousands of people in the city of Arecibo. Arecibo is also famous for its lighthouse and for its strong goat cheese.

The Arecibo Observatory is located about 35 miles (56 kilometers) from the city itself. A testament to modern technological wizardry, the observatory houses the world's largest radar-radio telescope. An enormous curved reflector spreads over

The entrance to Río Camuy Cave Park

a natural sinkhole, or karst, that is 300 feet (91 meters) deep and 1,300 feet (396 meters) across.

Not far from the observatory is the Río Camuy Cave Park, where visitors can explore one of the most extensive underground river systems in the world. A series of ramps and stairways leads into a network of caves carved out by ancient streams. In the dim light, stalagmites and stalactites give the caves a haunting, otherworldly appearance. Southeast of the park is Río Abajo State Forest, 5,800 acres (2,347 hectares) of primarily teak woodland.

The towns of Aguadilla and Aguada, on Puerto Rico's northwest corner, both claim to be the site of Columbus's landing in 1493. Since the claim has never been settled to their satisfaction, each honors the discoverer with a plaque.

The western port of Mayagüez is a center for trade and business. A series of bronze statues imported from Barcelona in the 1890s adorn the Plaza Colón. At the center of the plaza stands a statue of Christopher Columbus. Mayagüez is noted for fine needlework, and many shops sell handsome embroidered dresses, shawls, and linen. For a change of pace after the bustle of the city, visitors can explore the nearby Bosque Guajataca, a forest threaded with hiking trails.

The island of Mona, southwest of Puerto Rico, is a wildlife sanctuary open only to biologists and other serious students of natural history. Mona is a refuge for many species of seabirds and for the Puerto Rican iguana, which no longer survives in Puerto Rico itself.

The fishing village of La Parguera on Puerto Rico's southwest coast is a favorite resort for residents of San Juan. Houses perch above the water on stilts, and restaurants are renowned for their fine seafood. La Parguera is built on the shores of Phosphorescent Bay, one of Puerto Rico's most stunning natural attractions. Millions of tiny organisms in the water give off a strange luminous glow, turning the bay into a dazzling light show. On moonless nights, fishing boats take visitors out into the bay for a close-up view of this remarkable phenomenon.

The original settlement of San Germán stood on Puerto Rico's south coast. The village moved inland, however, after a series of attacks by pirates and other enemies. Today San Germán is a charming colonial town where, on Sunday nights, young men and women still dress up and circle around the plaza in the traditional courtship walk called the *paseo*. San Germán's Porta Coeli Church, built in 1593, is the second-oldest church in the Western Hemisphere. The oldest is the cathedral at Santo Domingo.

PONCE AND ITS ENVIRONS

Ponce is Puerto Rico's largest city outside the San Juan metropolitan area. The city was founded in honor of Ponce de

Ponce's attractions include the Cathedral of Our Lady of Guadelupe (left) and the Ponce Museum of Art (right)

León by Ponce's great-grandson in 1692. Ponce's central plaza, overshadowed by the majestic Cathedral of Our Lady of Guadelupe, is one of the loveliest town squares on the island. Gracing the plaza is a statue of Juan Morel Campos, Puerto Rico's beloved composer of *danza* tunes.

Just off the plaza stands the Ponce Museum of Art. It was designed by architect Edward Durell Stone, who also planned the Museum of Modern Art in New York City. The Ponce Museum has the finest collection of paintings in the Caribbean, displaying works by such European masters as Rubens, Van Dyck, Velázquez, and Courbet. The museum is especially noted for its collection of works by the nineteenth-century British artists known as the Pre-Raphaelites.

Ponce's Victorian firehouse is the most photographed building in Puerto Rico.

One sight that visitors to Ponce cannot miss is the Parque de Bombas, or firehouse. Created in 1883 to house an agricultural exposition, the firehouse is painted in exuberant red and black stripes and is adorned with green and yellow fanlights.

The Tibes Indian Ceremonial Center, just north of Ponce, offers a rare glimpse of life in Puerto Rico during the A.D. 700s. Seven ceremonial ball courts have been carefully excavated by archaeologists. A museum displays tools, weapons, jewelry, and other artifacts that have been found in the area. After touring Ponce's museums, the footsore traveler may relax at the nearby Baños de Coamo, a spa built over a natural hot spring.

Utuado is one of the most charming towns in the coffee-producing region north of Ponce. On its central plaza stand carved stones, or monoliths, that were decorated by the Arawak

Every year, horse lovers flock to Guayama for the Paso Fino Festival.

people of Borinquén about A.D. 1100. The monoliths are painted with geometric forms that were key symbols in Arawak religious practices.

The town of Jayuya is a paradise for anyone interested in traditional Puerto Rican crafts. Dozens of shops sell woven hammocks, straw hats, leather handbags, wooden maracas, and exquisite carved figures. Nearby, in the mountaintop village of Barranquitas, are the final resting places of Luis Muñoz Rivera and Luis Muñoz Marín, the father and son who dedicated their lives to Puerto Rican autonomy and development.

EASTERN PUERTO RICO

Among the delightful towns along Puerto Rico's southeast coast are Humacao and Guayama. Every March, horse lovers flock to Guayama for the Paso Fino Festival. Puerto Rico's *paso fino* horses, descended from sixteenth-century Spanish steeds, are bred to have an exceptionally even, flowing gait. Even at a gallop, these horses move so smoothly that a skilled rider can carry a glass of water without spilling a drop.

The town of Fajardo, at the eastern end of the island, is a major fishing and sailing center. Its three marinas berth thousands of small craft. Fajardo is the departure point for travelers who wish to ferry over to Puerto Rico's offshore islands of Vieques and Culebra.

Vieques is the site of a busy United States naval base, a source of controversy among the island's inhabitants. The island's largest town is Isabel Segunda, named for the Spanish queen who ruled in the mid-1800s. But the little fishing village of Esperanza, on Vieques' south coast, is more picturesque. About a hundred wild *paso fino* horses roam over the island.

About nine hundred people live on the tiny island of Culebra. Almost untouched by tourism and development, Culebra is a fine place for scuba diving and lobster fishing. Flamingo Bay, on the island's south coast, is ragged with coves and stippled with sandy islets.

El Yunque, part of the Caribbean National Forest, is the only tropical rain forest protected by the United States National Forest Service. Sprawling over some 28,000 acres (11,331 hectares) of mountain terrain, El Yunque is the habitat for some 240 species of plants and trees, only 6 of which are found on the United States mainland. Brightly colored birds dart through the foliage of moss-covered trees and sing from hiding places in tangles of vines. In 1989, Hurricane Hugo tore through El Yunque, uprooting everything in its path. But within a year, new vegetation sprang up from the wreckage, and the forest began to renew itself once more.

Probably the most familiar image of Puerto Rico, broadcast on postcards and travel brochures throughout the world, is sun-

Luquillo Beach is Puerto Rico's most famous beach.

drenched Luquillo Beach. Located some 30 miles (48 kilometers) east of San Juan, Luquillo is a year-round playground for families from the capital, as well as a resort for visitors to the island. At Luquillo, people of all ages lounge on the warm sand, sample mangoes and pineapples from vendors' carts, and play in the gentle waves.

Puerto Rico has seen tremendous changes during the twentieth century and faces the challenges of the future with optimism. As Governor Rafael Hernández Colón stated proudly, "Puerto Rico's most precious asset is its people. A proud people who have turned a beautiful island into a model for peace, progress, and democracy in the Caribbean."

FACTS AT A GLANCE

GENERAL INFORMATION

Official Name: Estado Libre Asociado de Puerto Rico (Commonwealth of Puerto Rico)

Became a Commonwealth: July 25, 1952

Origin of Name: *Puerto Rico* is Spanish for "rich port"

Capital: San Juan

Nickname: *Isla del Encanto* (Island of Enchantment)

Flag: The Puerto Rican flag has three red and two white horizontal stripes. A blue triangle with a white star in the center extends into the stripes.

Motto: *Joannes Est Nomen Eius,* Latin words meaning "John is his name"

Flower: *Maga*

Bird: *Reinita*

Tree: *Ceiba*

Animal: *Coquí* (a tree frog unique to Puerto Rico)

Song: "La Borinqueña," music by Felix Astol y Artés, lyrics by Manuel Fernandez Juncoz:

La tierra de Borinquén	The island of Borinquén
Donde he nacido yo	Where I was born
Es un jardín florido	Is a tropical garden
De mágico primor	Of magic splendor.
Un cielo siempre nítido	A sky that is always bright
Le sirve de dosel	It's like an enchanted canopy

Y dan arrullos plácidos	And sing pleasant lullabies
Las olas a sus pies	The waves on your feet.
Cuando a sus playas llegó Colón	When Columbus arrived
Exclamó llenó de admiración	Filled with admiration, he exclaimed:
¡Oh! ¡Oh! ¡Oh!	Oh! Oh! Oh!
Esta es la linda tierra	This is the beautiful land
Que busco yo	I'm looking for
Es Borinquén la hija	It's Borinquén, the daughter
La hija del mar y el sol	The daughter of the sea and sun
Del mar y el sol	The sea and sun
Del mar y el sol	The sea and sun

POPULATION

Population: 3,196,520 (1980 census)

Population Density: 909 people per sq. mi. (351 people per km²)

Population Distribution: About 67 percent of Puerto Ricans live in cities or towns. Most Puerto Ricans live in or around such large cities as San Juan, Bayamón, Ponce, Caguas, Arecibo, and Mayagüez.

San Juan	432,973
Bayamón	195,965
Ponce	188,219
Carolina	165,207
Caguas	118,020
Mayagüez	95,886
Arecibo	86,660
Guaynabo	80,857
Toa Baja	78,119
Aguadilla	52,627

(Population figures according to 1980 census)

Population Growth: Only 45,000 people (5,000 of them slaves) were found to be living in Puerto Rico when Major Alejandro O'Reilly conducted the first census in 1765. That number jumped to 332,000 in 1832, in part due to refugees from elsewhere in Latin America. Puerto Rico had about 1 million residents when Spain ceded Puerto Rico to the U.S. following the Spanish-American War. Since the turn of the century, Puerto Rico has experienced steady growth. After 1940, many Puerto Ricans migrated to cities on the U.S. mainland. That outflow reached 75,000 in 1953. The migration continued until about 1970. At that time, economic conditions on the mainland worsened, and many Puerto Ricans returned home. By 1975, the net inflow to the island reached 40,000 people. Puerto Rico also received many refugees in the 1960s as a result of revolutions in Cuba and the Dominican Republic. In 1980, Puerto Rico had more people than twenty-seven American states.

Year	Population
1900	953,753
1910	1,118,012
1920	1,299,809
1930	1,543,913
1940	1,869,255
1950	2,210,703
1960	2,349,544
1970	2,712,033
1980	3,196,520

GEOGRAPHY

Location: Puerto Rico is an island located between the Caribbean Sea and the Atlantic Ocean. It is the easternmost of the four large islands known as the Greater Antilles. The others are Cuba, Jamaica, and Hispaniola (shared by the nations of Haiti and the Dominican Republic).

Greatest Distances: East to west—111 mi. (179 km)
North to south—39 mi. (63 km)

Highest Point: Cerro de Punta, 4,389 ft. (1,338 m)

Lowest Point: Sea level, at the Caribbean Sea and Atlantic Ocean

Area: 3,515 sq. mi. (9,104 km²)

National Forests and Parklands: Puerto Ricans take pride in El Yunque rain forest in the eastern part of the island. This lush, 28,000-acre (11,331-hectare) forest, part of the Caribbean National Forest, contains about 3,355 species of plants and thousands of species of birds and animals. More than 100 billion gal. (379 billion l) of water fall on it each year. Puerto Rico also has three wildlife refuges covering a total of 2,425 acres (981 hectares).

Rivers: Puerto Rico has a number of rivers, all of which flow from sources in the Cordillera Central to the sea. Most of these rivers, including the Guajataca, Camuy, Arecibo, Toro Negro, Manatí, Cibuco, Plata, Bayamón, Guaynabo, and Loíza, flow north. The Anasco and Rosario flow west.

Lakes: Puerto Rico has no large natural lakes, but hydroelectric projects have dammed several rivers, creating artificial lakes. Cartagena, Guajataca, Carite, and Patillas are some of the larger lakes.

Coast: Puerto Rico's coastline measures 311 mi. (500 km). Including bays, inlets, and offshore islands, the shoreline runs about 700 mi. (1,127 km).

Jagüey Point reaches into the Caribbean between Salinas Bay and Sucia Bay in southwestern Puerto Rico.

Topography: Hills and mountains dominate the island of Puerto Rico. The chain of mountains known as the Cordillera Central forms a backbone through the middle of the island from east to west. Cerro de Punta, the island's highest mountain, is located in the western part of this chain. Foothills surround the central chain on the north and south. These smaller mountains contain many jagged peaks and rounded basins.

The coastal lowlands border the foothills on the north and south. Much of the island's sugarcane is grown in these low, humid areas. Coastal valleys on the eastern and western sides of the mountains provide sugarcane, coconuts, and other fruits.

Climate: Puerto Rico's agreeable climate makes it a year-round vacation spot. San Juan, on the north side of the island, has January temperatures ranging from 70° F. to 80° F. (21° C to 27° C) and July temperatures ranging from 76° F. to 84° F. (24° C to 29° C). Ponce, on the southern coast, experiences roughly the same temperatures. Because of their higher altitude, Puerto Rico's mountain regions tend to be cooler than those areas near the coast. The highest recorded temperature in Puerto Rico was 103° F. (39° C), at San Lorenzo on August 22, 1906. Puerto Rico's lowest temperature, 40° F. (4° C), was recorded at Aibonito on March 9, 1911.

Rain falls nearly every day in some regions, although the rainfall may last only a few minutes. The north averages about 70 in. (178 cm) of rain yearly, compared

Scuba divers enjoy the many species of colorful fish that swim near Puerto Rico's shores.

with about 37 in. (94 cm) in the south. Some regions, such as the El Yunque rain forest, may see more than 240 in. (610 cm) of rain per year.

Though Puerto Rico experiences mild weather throughout most of the year, hurricanes may devastate the island at any time from June through November, causing extensive loss of life and property damage. Extremely violent hurricanes strike about once every ten years.

NATURE

Trees: Mahogany, ebony, laurel, satinwood, *flamboyán* (poinciana), coconut palm, African tulip, jacaranda, *ceiba* (kapok), breadfruit, sea grape, star apple, *yagrumo*, butterfly tree, Spanish elm, Spanish cedar

Wild Plants: Bamboo, oleander, frangipani, mangrove, orchid, tree fern, bunchgrass, cactus, yucca, *maga*, poinsettia, bougainvillea, hibiscus, *canario*

Animals: Mongoose, bat, *coquí* (tree frog), iguana, lizard, mole cricket, termite, lobster, *cangrejo* (land crab), oyster, giant centipede, gecko

Birds: Nightingale, *gorrion*, thrush, oriole, grosbeak, *reinita*, *pitarre*, parrot, Puerto Rican pigeon, Puerto Rican whippoorwill, tanager, bullfinch, flycatcher, warbler, tern, plover, sandpiper

Fish: Barracuda, herring, marlin, red snapper, sailfish, mullet, pompano, shark, Spanish mackerel, tuna

Governor Raphael Hernández Colón

GOVERNMENT

Puerto Rico has a unique relationship with the U.S. It is neither a state nor a territory. Puerto Rican voters approved commonwealth status for their island in 1952. The island is self-governing, but the U.S. provides for its defense. Puerto Ricans are U.S. citizens who may travel freely in the U.S., work on the mainland, and serve in the armed forces. However, they do not pay federal income tax. Puerto Ricans send delegates to American political conventions, but they may not vote in U.S. presidential elections while living in Puerto Rico (although they may cast their votes if living on the mainland). Puerto Rico's voters elect a resident commissioner to sit in the U.S. House of Representatives. He or she may vote in committees but not on final legislation in the House.

Although a 1967 plebiscite showed that most Puerto Ricans approved of commonwealth status, there are those on the island who would like to see change. Some would like Puerto Rico to become an independent nation. Others desire to see it join the Union as the fifty-first state. If Puerto Rico became a state, it would be entitled to two U.S. senators, about six members of the House of Representatives, and about eight electoral votes in presidential elections.

Like the federal government, Puerto Rico's government has three branches. The governor, elected by the people every four years, heads the executive branch. The governor appoints other executive officials.

The legislative branch, or legislative assembly, consists of a senate and a house of representatives. Members of the legislative assembly are elected from eight

Puerto Rico's capitol building

senatorial districts (with two senators each) and forty representative districts. The total number of legislators varies from election to election. Puerto Rican law allows minority-party representation even if that party is defeated in every district. The legislature may add extra members to accommodate those minority parties.

Puerto Rico's governor appoints the eight members of the supreme court, the highest court in Puerto Rico's judicial system. Supreme-court justices serve twelve-year terms and may serve until they reach the age of seventy. The ninety-two superior-court judges serve twelve-year terms, and the ninety-nine district-court judges are elected to eight-year terms.

There are no county or town governments in Puerto Rico. Instead, the island is divided into seventy-eight *municipios* (municipalities). Each elects a mayor and an assembly.

Number of Municipalities: 78

U.S. Representatives: One nonvoting resident commissioner

Electoral Votes: 0

Voting Qualifications: U.S. citizen, registered to vote fifty days before election (Puerto Ricans living on the U.S. mainland must comply with the voting qualifications of their current state of residence)

EDUCATION

When the United States claimed Puerto Rico as a territory in 1898, more than three of every four Puerto Ricans could not read or write. To address this, an extensive public school system was instituted. Today, more than 90 percent of Puerto Ricans are literate. Until 1930, U.S. authorities insisted upon using English as the language of instruction. That rule met strong and successful opposition from the islanders. Today, Spanish is taught as the basic language, but all students study English as well.

The University of Puerto Rico, which has its main campus at Río Piedras, is the largest institution of higher learning in Puerto Rico. The university also includes campuses at Mayagüez, San Juan, Cayey, and Humacao, as well as several regional colleges. Other schools include American College of Puerto Rico, Bayamón Central University, and Caribbean University College, all in Bayamón; Antillian College, in Mayagüez; Catholic University of Puerto Rico, at Ponce; the Center for Advanced Studies on Puerto Rico and the Caribbean, at San Juan; the Conservatory of Music of Puerto Rico, the University of the Sacred Heart, and the Caribbean Center for Advanced Studies, all in Santurce; Ana G. Mendez Educational Foundation, at Caguas; and Inter American University of Puerto Rico, which has campuses in Hato Rey and San Germán.

ECONOMY AND INDUSTRY

Principal Products:
Agriculture: Sugarcane, coffee, tobacco, cotton, dairy products, beef cattle, bananas, avocados, pineapples, plantains, citrus fruits, coconuts, poultry, beans, vegetables, honey, rice

Manufacturing: Chemicals, processed foods, electrical products, metal products, textiles and clothing, Panama hats, tobacco products, scientific instruments, stone, clay, and glass products

Natural Resources: Sand, gravel, stone, clay, manganese, copper, nickel, cobalt

Business and Trade: Small farming provided most of the income throughout much of Puerto Rico's history. After World War II, however, the economy underwent great changes. An ambitious economic self-help program called Operation Bootstrap boosted the island's net income from $225 million in 1940 to $5.7 billion in 1974. In the process, Puerto Rico was converted from an agricultural economy to a manufacturing economy.

Sugarcane is still the leading agricultural product, followed by coffee and tobacco. About 60 percent of Puerto Rico's land is used as farmland.

The U.S. remains Puerto Rico's major trading partner, although the island also imports a significant amount of oil from Venezuela. Puerto Ricans do not pay duties on goods imported from the U.S. San Juan, Ponce, and Mayagüez are the island's main ports. Mayagüez enjoys a duty-free zone.

Communication: *La Gaceta de Puerto Rico,* Puerto Rico's first newspaper, appeared in 1807. Today, three major papers, all published in San Juan, are

A Puerto Rican coffee grower

distributed throughout the island. They are *El Nuevo Día, El Vocero,* and the English-language *San Juan Star.* WKAQ, the island's first radio station, began airing from San Juan in 1922. Its companion television station, WKAQ-TV, began broadcasting in 1954. Today, Puerto Rico has about one hundred radio stations and ten television stations.

Transportation: A good system of roads crisscrosses the island, allowing for automobiles, trucks, and an excellent public bus system. Puerto Rico has more than 7,000 mi. (11,265 km) of paved roads and highways. Because it is an island, Puerto Rico relies heavily on air travel. Eighteen airports, twelve heliports, and a seaplane base provide air service. Puerto Rico International Airport in San Juan, the island's major airport, offers flights to and from the United States, West Indies, and Europe.

SOCIAL AND CULTURAL LIFE

Museums: Puerto Ricans take pride in their heritage, and they display that heritage in museums. At the University of Puerto Rico in Río Piedras is the Museum of Anthropology, History and Art, which displays hundreds of exhibits on Puerto Rico's archaeological and cultural history. The San Juan Museum of Art and History features exhibits of Puerto Rican art and an audiovisual history of San Juan. Also in San Juan are the Casa del Libro (House of the Book), which contains a

The Pablo Casals Museum in San Juan (left) honors famed cellist and composer Pablo Casals (right).

huge collection of valuable old manuscripts as well as modern graphic works; the Pablo Casals Museum, which houses memorabilia of the famed cellist; the Museum of Colonial Architecture, which displays blueprints, city plans, and photographs; the Museum of Santos, which offers many fine examples of the small wooden religious figures for which the island is famous; and the Pharmacy Museum, a nineteenth-century pharmacy housed in the city's oldest house. San Juan also has many fine art galleries that feature changing exhibits.

The Ponce Museum of Art, housed in a building designed by famed architect Edward Durell Stone, has the finest collection of European paintings in the Caribbean. Another interesting museum is the Museum of the Conquest and Colonization of Puerto Rico at Caparra Ruins, outside Bayamón. The Marine Station Museum in Mayagüez displays many Caribbean specimens.

Libraries: The Ateneo Puertorriqueño has a library of Puerto Rican culture in San Juan. The Volunteer Library League in San Juan contains an excellent bilingual library. The Teachers Association also boasts a fine library. Lions clubs throughout the island fund libraries in smaller towns.

Performing Arts: One man more than any other is responsible for making Puerto Rico an international center for classical music. Famed cellist and composer Pablo Casals moved to Puerto Rico—his mother's homeland—from Spain in 1956. He helped create a first-class symphony orchestra in San Juan—the Puerto Rico Symphony Orchestra—and founded the Puerto Rican Conservatory of Music, which provides training for serious musicians. The annual Pablo Casals Festival, first organized by Casals in 1957, attracts world-renowned classical musicians.

Puerto Ricans may enjoy many other cultural performances as well. The Department of Parks and Recreation presents Spanish-language plays and gives courses on music, folk dancing, and drama. The Tapia Theater, in Old San Juan, provides a major showcase for visiting performers. The San Juan City Ballet performs in Old San Juan. The Areyto Folklore group performs traditional folk dances.

Puerto Rico's multiethnic heritage has created a rich and varied musical tradition that includes Latin, African, Caribbean, and American influences. Out of these influences have arisen such captivating musical forms as the *danza, décima,* and *plena.* In recent years, Puerto Rico has become famous for the zesty music known as *salsa.*

Sports and Recreation: Puerto Ricans are baseball fanatics. Many major leaguers spend the off-season perfecting their skills in the six-team Puerto Rican winter league. Baseball stadiums stand in San Juan, Santurce, Ponce, Caguas, Arecibo, and Mayagüez.

Former Pittsburgh Pirates Hall of Famer Roberto Clemente, a humanitarian as well as an outstanding baseball player, became a national hero. He built a large sports complex in San Juan that is now used by thousands of boys and girls. Throughout the island, people play baseball, basketball, golf, and tennis. Boxing is another popular sporting event. El Comandante Racetrack, in Canóvanas, is an attractive, modern facility that features some of the finest horses and jockeys. Cockfighting is popular, especially in the smaller towns. Along the coast, people enjoy sailing, surfing, snorkeling, and scuba diving. Deep-sea fishing has become a booming sport in Puerto Rico.

Historic Sites and Landmarks:

Casa Blanca, in San Juan, is the oldest house in Puerto Rico. Built in 1521 for Ponce de León and owned by his family until the late 1700s, it now serves as a museum and cultural center.

Casa de los Contrafuertes (Buttress House) is one of the oldest houses in San Juan, dating from the early 1700s. It houses the Pharmacy Museum and a graphic-arts museum.

Cathedral of San Juan Bautista, in San Juan, contains the tomb of Ponce de León. Last rebuilt in 1802, the cathedral still preserves Gothic detailing dating from 1540.

Fort San Gerónimo, in San Juan, withstood a 1797 British attack and now houses a Spanish military museum.

La Fortaleza, in San Juan, is Spain's earliest fort, completed in 1540. Today, it serves as the official residence of Puerto Rico's governor.

Cueva del Indio, near Arecibo, is a cave that served as a place of worship for Indians before the arrival of the Spaniards. Ancient cave paintings are still visible on the cave's walls.

El Morro, in San Juan, is a massive fortress that was built by the Spanish to guard San Juan against foreign raiders. Begun in 1539, it was not completed until 1783.

San Juan Cathedral

Muñoz Rivera Home, in Barranquitas, was the longtime residence of famed Puerto Rican statesman Luis Muñoz Rivera.

Porta Coeli, in San Germán, is a distinguished chapel dating from 1606. Today, it houses a museum of religious art.

San José Church, in San Juan, was built in 1523, making it one of the oldest churches in the Western Hemisphere.

Tibes Indian Ceremonial Center, near Ponce, is the site of the oldest cemetery yet uncovered in the Antilles. On display are excavated human skeletons that date back to A.D. 300, seven ceremonial ballparks, and a replica of a Taíno village.

Other Interesting Places to Visit:

Las Américas Expressway, between San Juan and Ponce, weaves through some of Puerto Rico's highest mountains.

Arecibo Ionospheric Observatory, near Arecibo, contains a giant radar-radio telescope.

Tibes Indian Ceremonial Center, near Ponce

Botanical Garden, in Río Piedras, includes a thick forest, lotus lagoon, bamboo promenade, and orchid garden.

El Capitolio, in San Juan, is an imposing, white, classical-style capitol building.

Condado, in San Juan, is a lively beachfront area filled with restaurants, hotels, nightclubs, and fashionable shops.

Luquillo Beach, east of San Juan, is considered Puerto Rico's finest beach.

Mayagüez Zoo, in Mayagüez, has more than five hundred species of birds and animals.

Panoramic Route, from Yabucoa to Mayagüez, passes through breathtaking mountain scenery.

Parque de Bombas, in Ponce, is a red-and-black Victorian firehouse that is the most photographed building in Puerto Rico.

Phosphorescent Bay, near Parguera, glows and shimmers on dark nights because of tiny luminescent creatures that live in the water.

San Germán, built in 1573, has retained the look and feel of a small, Spanish town.

Torrecilla Baja, near Loíza, is a large mangrove swamp that includes a large bird sanctuary.

El Yunque, in northeastern Puerto Rico, is a lush, rain-forest-covered mountain that features hundreds of species of plants, trees, and birds.

IMPORTANT DATES

c. A.D. 1 — The Igneri people, known for their beautiful and exotic pottery designs, inhabit Puerto Rico

c. 1000 — The Taínos, an Arawak people, reach Puerto Rico

1493 — On his second trip to the New World, Christopher Columbus, sailing for Spain, reaches Puerto Rico; he names the island San Juan Bautista

1508 — At a site across the bay from present-day San Juan, Juan Ponce de León establishes Caparra, the first European settlement on the island

1511 — The Taínos rebel against their enslavement by the Spanish, but fall to Spanish forces led by Ponce de León

1513 — Spain authorizes the importation of African slaves

1521 — San Juan becomes the capital of Puerto Rico

1532 — Construction begins on La Fortaleza, a fortress overlooking San Juan Bay and intended as a house for Ponce de León

1539 — Work begins on El Morro, a fortress located on the tip of the San Juan Peninsula

1544 — Fewer than one hundred Arawak Indians remain from a group that had numbered about thirty thousand when the Spaniards first came to Puerto Rico

1545 — Puerto Rico becomes ruled by judge-governors chosen by the Spanish king or the *Audiencia* of Santo Domingo

1595 — Sir Francis Drake attacks Puerto Rico, but is repelled

1598 — The English capture San Juan and hold it for several months

1625 — The Dutch burn San Juan, but eventually are forced to retreat

1702 — The English sack Arecibo

1736 — Coffee is introduced to Puerto Rico

1765 — Marshall Alejandro O'Reilly visits the island and makes a detailed report to the Spanish Crown on its conditions

1788 — Fray Iñigo Abad y Lasierra writes the first published history of the island

1797 — The British, led by Ralph Abercromby, attack San Juan but are repelled

The Ponce market in the 1890s

1808 — Napoleon Bonaparte of France invades Spain and deposes the Spanish king; wanting to keep Puerto Rico loyal to Spain, the Spanish government-in-exile invites Puerto Rico to send a delegate, Ramón Power y Giralt, to the Spanish *Cortes* (assembly)

1810 — Thousands of Spanish loyalists immigrate to Puerto Rico from Mexico and South America

1812 — Through his participation in the *Cortes,* Ramón Power helps win such reforms as the passage of a new, more liberal Spanish constitution, Spanish citizenship for Puerto Ricans, and tax reforms

1814 — The restoration of King Ferdinand II to the Spanish throne marks the return of absolute rule to Puerto Rico and the loss of Spanish citizenship for Puerto Ricans

1815 — Spain allows Puerto Rican trade and immigration with nations other than Spain

1849 — Manuel Alonso publishes *El gíbaro,* an important book describing peasant life in Puerto Rico

1868 — In the revolt that becomes known as *El Grito de Lares* (The Shout of Lares), rebels proclaim Puerto Rico an independent republic; the revolt is put down by troops sent by the Spanish governor

1876 — The Ateneo Puertorriqueño, an important cultural institution, opens

1897 — Spain allows Puerto Rico to form an autonomous government

1898 — U.S. troops land in Puerto Rico; Puerto Rico is ceded to the U.S. in the aftermath of the Spanish-American War

1900 — President William McKinley appoints the first American colonial governor under the newly passed Foraker Act, which sets up a government for the island run almost entirely by the U.S. Congress

1903 — The University of Puerto Rico at Río Piedras is established as a normal (teachers') school

1917 — Puerto Ricans become American citizens under the Jones Act

1928 — Hurricane San Felipe devastates Puerto Rico, leaving 500,000 people destitute and causing an estimated $85 million in property damage

1937 — In what becomes known as the Ponce Massacre, twenty-one people are killed and about one hundred are wounded when police stop a Nationalist party parade in Ponce on Palm Sunday

1946 — President Harry S. Truman appoints Jesús T. Piñero as the first native-born Puerto Rican governor

1947 — Congress amends the Jones Act to allow Puerto Ricans to elect their own governor

1948 — Luis Muñoz Marín takes office as the first elected governor of Puerto Rico

1949 — The Caribe Hilton, the island's first luxury hotel, opens

1950 — President Truman signs the Constitution Act, granting Puerto Rico status as a U.S. commonwealth and allowing Puerto Rico to design its own government based on its own constitution; two Puerto Rican nationalists attempt an assault on Blair House, the temporary residence of President Truman

1952 — Puerto Rico becomes a U.S. commonwealth

1954 — Four Puerto Rican nationalists shoot and wound five congressmen in the chamber of the U.S. House of Representatives

1961 — The *San Juan Star* wins a Pulitzer Prize

1967 — Puerto Ricans vote to remain a commonwealth

1972 — Baseball star and national hero Roberto Clemente perishes in a plane crash while on a mission of mercy to Nicaraguan earthquake victims

1985 — A three-day rainstorm causes a mudslide that kills 150 people in Ponce

1989 — Hurricane Hugo ravages Puerto Rico, causing extensive damage and loss of life

IMPORTANT PEOPLE

Fray Iñigo Abad y Lasierra (1745-1813), religious leader, journalist; secretary of the bishop of Puerto Rico; wrote *Historia geográfica, civil, y natural de la Isla de San Juan Bautista de Puerto Rico*, the first history of the island

Pedro Albizu Campos (1893-1965), born in Ponce; politician; favored dominion status based on Canadian government, but later advocated Puerto Rican independence, including violent revolution

PEDRO ALBIZU CAMPOS

Fray Juan Alejo de Arizmendi (1760-1814), born in San Juan; first Puerto Rican bishop; appointed to the See of San Juan

Manuel A. Alonso y Pacheco (1822-1899), born in San Juan; physician, author; wrote *El gíbaro*, a book on the mores and traditions of rural Puerto Rican society that is considered the first great Puerto Rican book; led a group of expatriate Puerto Rican writers in Spain; wrote many books describing Puerto Rican customs

Francisco J. Amy (1837-1912), born in Arroyo; author; founded the literary magazine *El Estudio* with Manuel Zeno Gandía; published *La Gaceta Ilustrada*, one of the first major Spanish-language publications in New York City; wrote in English and Spanish and translated works from authors in both languages

MANUEL ALONSO

HERMAN BADILLO

RAMÓN E. BETANCES

RÓMULO BETANCOURT

PABLO CASALS

Bailey K. Ashford (1873-1934), soldier, doctor; served as an army surgeon in Puerto Rico during the Spanish American War; discovered and helped eradicate hookworm disease in Puerto Rico

Felix Astol y Artés (1813-1901), musician; wrote the music for "La Borinqueña," the Puerto Rican national anthem

Herman Badillo (1929-　　), born in Caguas; politician; won election as Bronx borough president but lost 1969 mayoral election in New York City; U.S. representative from New York (1971-77); first native-born Puerto Rican to serve in Congress

Antonio R. Barceló (1868-1938), born in Fajardo; journalist, orator; led the Union party after Muñoz Rivera's death; served in the chamber of delegates (1906-14); president of Puerto Rican senate (1917-30); founded the Alliance party (1924)

Ramón Emeterio Betances (1827-1898), born in Cabo Rojo; physician, social reformer; led efforts to abolish the 1855 cholera epidemic; led crusade to abolish slavery; led the separatist movement that resulted in *El Grito de Lares*

Rómulo Betancourt (1908-1981); Venezuelan statesman; lived in exile in Puerto Rico before being elected president of Venezuela in 1958; led democracy movement in Venezuela; became the first president in Venezuelan history to serve a complete term, then pass the reins of government to his successor; initiated land and education reforms while president

Maria Cadilla de Martínez (1884?-1951), born in Arecibo; essayist, folklorist; won prizes from the Ateneo Puertorriqueño for her folklore and legends (1946) and her paintings (1947); wrote *Poesia popular en Puerto Rico* (*Popular Poetry in Puerto Rico*) and *Juegos y canciones infantiles de Puerto Rico* (*Children's Games and Songs of Puerto Rico*)

José Campeche (1752-1809), born in San Juan; artist; painted many portraits but was best known for his religious works; created the main altar of the Church of Santa Ana in San Juan

Nemesio R. Canales (1878-1923), born in Jayuya; author, critic; wrote *Paliques*, a collection of articles about literature, philosophy, and social criticism; founded the weekly satirical paper *Juan Bobo*; wrote a novel, *Mi voluntad ha muerto* (*My Will Is Gone*); gained fame as a humorist

Pablo Casals (1876-1973), born Pau Carlos Salvador Defillo de Casals; cellist, composer, conductor; moved to Puerto Rico (his mother's homeland) in 1956; was considered the greatest cellist of his time; helped make the Puerto Rican Symphony a major musical force and rejuvenated interest in classical music and arts; inaugurated the annual Casals festival; composed the oratorio *El pesebre* (*The Manger*)

José Celso Barbosa (1857-1921), born in Bayamón; physician, politician, editor; founded the Statehood Republican party of Puerto Rico (1899); favored U.S. annexation of Puerto Rico and ultimate statehood

Orlando Cepeda (1937-   ), born in Ponce; professional baseball player; helped lead the San Francisco Giants to a National League pennant in 1962; led the National League in home runs and runs batted in during the 1961 season

Ferdinand R. Cestero (1864-1945), born in San Juan; poet; influenced many of the poets of Latin America's modernist movement; wrote *Ave populi* (*Hail to the People*) and *Lirica: pagina azul* (*Lyric: Blue Page*); wrote such children's poems as "Los munecas hablan" ("The Dolls Talk") and "Flores y alas" ("Flowers and Wings")

FERDINAND CESTERO

Roberto Walker Clemente (1934-1972), born in Carolina; professional baseball player; achieved 3,000 major-league hits; won four National League batting championships; was named National League Most Valuable Player in 1966; led Pittsburgh Pirates to two World Series wins; earned respect as one of best all-around players in history; died in a plane crash while flying to Nicaragua to help earthquake victims

Christopher Columbus (1451-1506), explorer; discovered the New World of the Western Hemisphere while seeking a western route to Asia; discovered Puerto Rico while on his second voyage to the New World (1493)

ROBERTO CLEMENTE

Gilberto Concepción de Gracia (1909-1968), born in Vega Alta; politician; founded the Puerto Rican Independence party (1945); wrote *The Land Authority of Puerto Rico*

José Cruz (1947-   ), born in Arroyo; professional baseball player; as an outfielder, helped lead the Houston Astros into the playoffs three times; hit .300 or better six times and retired with more than 2,000 career hits

CHRISTOPHER COLUMBUS

Virgilio Dávila (1869-1943), born in Toa Baja; teacher, farmer, poet; wrote *Patria* (*Homeland*), an epic poem dealing with landscape, love, and the lives of famous people; in *Viviendo y amando* (*Living and Loving*), adopted the modernist poetry of Rubén Dario; described customs of the late 1800s in *Pueblito de antes* (*Little Town of Long Ago*)

Osiris Delgado (1920-   ), born in Humacao; artist; was influenced by Spanish classic styles; employed bright tropical colors and Puerto Rican themes; served as president of Fine Arts section of the Ateneo Puertorriqueño and director of the Museum of Anthropology, History, and Art of the University of Puerto Rico

JOSÉ CRUZ

JOSÉ DE DIEGO

JOSÉ FELICIANO

LUIS FERRÉ

JOSÉ FERRER

Abelardo Díaz Alfaro (1920-   ), born in Caguas; social worker, writer; wrote the immensely popular book *Terrazo*, a collection of stories of rural life

José de Diego (1867-1918), born in Aguadilla; poet, orator, politician; became the first speaker of the house of delegates under the Foraker Act; advocated Puerto Rican independence; led the fight for the teaching of Spanish in Puerto Rico's schools; wrote *Cantos de rebeldia* (*Songs of Rebellion*)

Manuel Elzaburu (1852-1892), born in San Juan; essayist, critic; wrote under the pseudonym Fabián Montes; founded the Ateneo Puertorriqueño; introduced prose poems to Puerto Rico; wrote *Relaciones de la literature con la historia de los pueblos* (*Relationship of Literature to the History of Peoples*)

José Feliciano (1945-   ), born in Lares; musician; virtuoso guitar player; won two Grammy awards; sang "Light My Fire" and the theme from "Chico and the Man"

Luis Ferré (1904-   ), born in Ponce; politician; governor of Puerto Rico (1969-73); was governor during a time of heated debate between pro-commonwealth and pro-statehood forces; helped found the Ponce Museum of Art

José Ferrer (1912-   ), born in Santurce; actor; won an Academy award for his portrayal of the title role in *Cyrano de Bergerac* (1950); also appeared in such films as *The Caine Mutiny*, *Whirlpool*, and *Ship of Fools*; produced and directed *Stalag 13* on Broadway

José Gautier Benítez (1848-1880), born in Caguas or Humacao; soldier, poet; wrote *El progreso* (*Progress*) under the pseudonym Gustavo; wrote *Canto a Puerto Rico* (*Song to Puerto Rico*); wrote romantic poems about Puerto Rico

José Polonio Hernández (1892-1922), born in Hatillo; poet known as Peache; wrote *Copias de la vereda* (*Couplets of the Path*); composed poems acclaimed for their vision of nature; published *El ultimo combate* (*The Last Combat*)

Rafael Hernández (1898-1965), born in Aguadilla; composer; wrote music known and acclaimed throughout Latin America; composed sentimental songs, hymns, rumbas, boleros, zarzuelas, and opera music; organized the Borinquen Trio in New York; famous songs include "Preciosa," ("Precious"), "Nada es verdad" ("Nothing is True") and "Canto para ti" ("Song for You")

Eugenio María de Hostos (1839-1903), born near Mayagüez; writer, abolitionist, educator; sought a federation of free West Indies countries

Juan Ramón Jimenez (1881-1958); author; lived in Puerto Rico from 1951 until his death; won the 1956 Nobel Prize for literature for his lyrical poetry; wrote *Belleza* (*Beauty*) and *Animal de fondo* (*Animal of the Depth*)

Raul Julia (1940-   ), born in San Juan; actor; starred in such films as *Kiss of the Spider Woman* and *Presumed Innocent*; won four Tony nominations for his work on Broadway; appeared in plays as diverse as *Where's Charley?, Threepenny Opera*, and *Dracula*

RAUL JULIA

Luis Lloréns Torres (1876-1944), born in Collores; poet, essayist; wrote *Al pie de la Alhambra* (*At the Foot of the Alhambra*); founded and directed the satiric weekly *Juan Bobo* with Nemesio Canales: wrote the symbolist poem *La canción de las Antillas* (*Song of the Antilles*); published the historical drama *El grito de Lares*

Francisco (Paquito) Lopez Cruz (1909-1988), born in Naranjito; guitarist, teacher; composed such songs as "Si tu fueras rosa" ("If You Were a Rose"); taught music and folklore for many years at the University of Puerto Rico and wrote several books about Puerto Rican folklore; gained renown for both classical and modern guitar playing

PAQUITO LOPEZ CRUZ

Antonio de los Reyes Correa (?-1758), soldier; in 1702, repelled an English attack at San Juan despite the superior arms of the English forces

René Marqués (1919-   ), playwright, novelist, essayist; one of Puerto Rico's best-known contemporary writers; wrote the humorous play *Juan bobo y la dama del Occidente* (*Foolish Juan and the Lady from the West*)

Rosendo Matienzo Cintrón (1855-1913), born in Luquillo; attorney, social reformer; fought for abolition of the death penalty, creation of savings cooperatives, and preservation of Puerto Rican lands for Puerto Ricans; formed the Union of Puerto Rico, a progressive nonpartisan group; founded the Independence party (1912)

RENÉ MARQUÉS

Concha Meléndez (1895-   ), born in Caguas; poet, essayist, literary critic; published more than twenty books, as well as many studies and articles; won respect as one of the outstanding authorities on Latin American literature; wrote *La novela hispanoamericana* (*The Hispanic-American Novel*)

Angel Mislán (1862-1911), born in San Sebastián; musician; played the clarinet and French horn; directed dance orchestras; composed waltzes, mazurkas, *pasadobles*, and *jíbaro* songs; wrote two of the best-known Puerto Rican *danzas*: "Sara," and "Tu y Yo" ("You and I")

Juan Morel Campos (1857-1896), born in Ponce; musician; played the flute, French horn, and counterbass; known as the father of the *danza*; made Ponce a musical center when he founded the Fireman's Band of Ponce; famous works include "No me toques" ("Don't Touch Me") and "Laura y Georgina"; wrote the symphony *Puerto Rico* and the march *Juegos flores* (*Floral Games*); wrote many *zarzuelas* (musical plays)

CONCHA MELÉNDEZ

RITA MORENO

LUIS MUÑOZ MARÍN

HERNÁN PADILLA

ANTONIO PAOLI

Rita Moreno (1931-   ), born in Humacao; actress, dancer, singer; has appeared in many plays and films; has received many entertainment awards, including an Academy award for her role in *West Side Story*; a Tony award for her role in the Broadway play *The Ritz*; a Grammy for the music from the television program "The Electric Company," and Emmy awards for appearances on "The Muppet Show" and "The Rockford Files"

Luis Muñoz Marín (1898-1980), born in San Juan; politician; founded the Popular Democratic party (1938); president of Puerto Rico's senate (1940-48); first elected governor of Puerto Rico (1948-64); helped develop Operation Bootstrap; helped devise the commonwealth relationship with the U.S. put into effect in 1952

Luis Muñoz Rivera (1859-1916), born in Barranquitas; journalist, politician; father of Luis Muñoz Marín; founded the newspaper *La Democracia* (1889); led the movement that attained for Puerto Rico the Autonomic Charter in 1897; headed the cabinet that took office in 1898; resident commissioner to the U.S. Congress (1911-16)

Demeterio O'Daly (1780-1837), born in San Juan; soldier; fought despotic Spanish King Ferdinando VII in 1814; defended the Puente de Matamulas (Bridge of Matamulas) despite orders to abandon it if the enemy had a superior force

Francisco Oller y Cesteros (1833-1917), born in Bayamón; artist; became known as one of Puerto Rico's finest painters; invested his work with his sense of social values; painted such famous works as *Las Tinieblas* (*Darkness*) and *Colón Encadenado* (*Columbus Chained*); advocated the abolition of slavery in his paintings; painted more than eight hundred works, many of which were of huge dimensions

Hernán Padilla (1938-   ), born in San Juan; politician; first Hispanic American elected to head the U.S. Conference of Mayors (1984)

Luis Palés Matos (1898-1959), born in Guayama; poet; founded the magazine El Pueblo (*The People*); wrote poems that exalted Puerto Rico's African heritage; famous poems include "Pueblo negro" ("Black Town") and "Danzarina africana" ("African Dance")

Antonio Paoli (1872-1946), born in Ponce; singer; starred at Milan's Scala opera house as the first great tenor to sing Rossini's *William Tell*; stunned audiences with his performances in the Verdi operas *Otello* and *Trovatore*; performed throughout Europe and South America; won fame as "The Tenor of Kings and the King of Tenors"

Victor Pellor (1931-   ), born in Arecibo; professional baseball player; thrilled fans with his slick fielding for the Kansas City Athletics and Cleveland Indians; hit .300 or better in three seasons

Jesús T. Piñero (1897-1952), born in Carolina; politician; in 1946, became the first Puerto Rican to be appointed governor of the island by a U.S. president; held many government positions; worked to improve sugarcane and livestock production

Juan Ponce de León (1460?-1521), Spanish explorer; best known for his search for the Fountain of Youth; explored and colonized Puerto Rico in 1508; built Caparra, Puerto Rico's first European settlement; governor of the island (1509); the city of Ponce is named in his honor

JUAN PONCE DE LEÓN

Ramón Power y Giralt (1775-1813), politician; represented Puerto Rico in the Spanish *Cortes*; participated in the drafting of the Spanish constitution of 1812; led liberal reforms

Tito Puente (1923-   ), musician; played saxophone, clarinet, and many percussion instruments; popularized Latin music on the American mainland; composed more than two hundred songs and became known as "El Rey" ("The King") of big-band mambo

TITO PUENTE

Francisco Mariano Quiñones (1830-1908), born in San Germán; social reformer; sought the end of slavery in Puerto Rico; served as president of the brief autonomous government of 1897; later served as official historian of Puerto Rico; wrote two novels and many plays

José Ignacio Quintón (1881-1925), born in Caguas; pianist, composer; composed two masses, as well as marches, quartets, and trios; created many *danzas*, such as "El coquí," "Tus ojos" ("Your Eyes"), "Adelaida," and "Si tu fueras mia" ("If You Were Mine")

Alejandro Ramírez (1777-1821), agriculturalist; introduced agricultural and industrial machinery to the island; published a business periodical, *Diario económico de Puerto Rico* (*Economic Diary of Puerto Rico*)

FRANCISCO QUIÑONES

Felisa Rincón de Gautier (1897-   ), born in San Juan; politician; mayor of San Juan (1946-68); was named Woman of the Year in the Americas for 1954, the year she presided over the Inter-American Organization of Municipalities

Lola Rodríguez de Tío (1854-1924), born in San Germán; poet; wrote patriotic lyrics that were adapted for the national anthem; wrote *Mis Cantares* (*My Songs*), a collection of twenty-five hundred poems; sought to liberate pro-independence writers held captive and wrote "Nochebuena" ("Christmas Eve") upon their release

Luis Rodríguez Miranda (1875-1949), born in Utuado; clarinetist, composer; wrote many kinds of musical compositions, including *danzas* and mazurkas

FELISA RINCÓN DE GAUTIER

AGUSTÍN STAHL

MANUEL ZENO GANDÍA

Ana Roqué de Duprey (1853-1933), born in Aguadilla; writer, social reformer; founded several magazines; wrote *Pasatiempos* (*Pastimes*), *Novels y cuentos* (*Novels and Stories*) and *Luz y sombra* (*Light and Shadow*); led the *Asociación Puertorriqueña de mujeres sufragistas* (Puerto Rican Association for Women's Suffrage)

Segundo Ruiz Belvis (1829-1867), born in Hormigueros; statesman; founded Puerto Rico's Abolition Society; served as delegate to Spanish session designed to provide some autonomy for Puerto Rico and Cuba; died mysteriously in Chile while enlisting Chilean aid for Puerto Rican autonomy

Jesús Maria Sanromá (1902-   ), born in Carolina; pianist; performed in concerts in Europe, South America, and the U.S.; directed piano studies at the Conservatory of Music in Hato Rey

Agustín Stahl (1842-1917), born in Aguadilla; scientist, physician; wrote a much-acclaimed study of diphtheria for his doctoral thesis; studied and wrote about many natural sciences, including zoology, botany, medicine, and anthropology; opened a natural-history museum

Alejandro Tapia y Rivera (1826-1882), born in San Juan; author; wrote history, drama, poetry, and literary criticism; founded and directed the Philharmonic Society

Miguel Xiorro y Velazco (1743-1801), born in San Juan; philanthropist; donated his entire fortune to schools and seminaries in San Juan

Manuel Zeno Gandía (1855-1930), born in Arecibo; novelist; journalist, poet, historian; edited scientific and literary journals; wrote an acclaimed study of pre-Columbian culture; wrote the novel *La charca* (The Pond)

COMMONWEALTH GOVERNORS

Luis Muñoz Marín	1948-1964
Roberto Sánchez Vilella	1964-1968
Luis Ferré	1968-1972
Rafael Hernández Colón	1972-1976
Carlos Romero Barceló	1976-1984
Rafael Hernández Colón	1984-

Topography

From *New International World Atlas* © 1990 by Rand McNally, R.L. 90-S-90

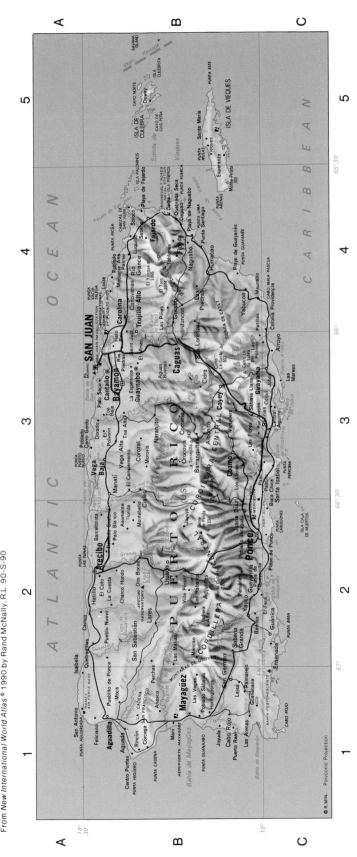

© R. MCN. Polyconic Projection

VEGETABLES	PINEAPPLES
TOBACCO	HONEY
COTTON	RICE
DAIRY PRODUCTS	MINING
PEANUTS	BEANS
MANUFACTURING	FRUIT
POULTRY	CORN
SUGARCANE	BEEF
YAMS	COFFEE
COCONUTS	

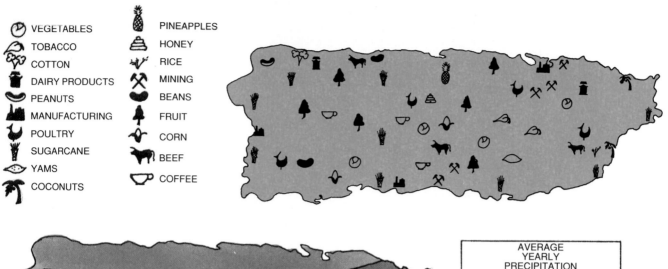

AVERAGE YEARLY PRECIPITATION

Centimeters		Inches
254 to 508		100 to 200
203 to 254		80 to 100
102 to 203		40 to 80
51 to 102		20 to 40

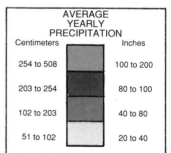

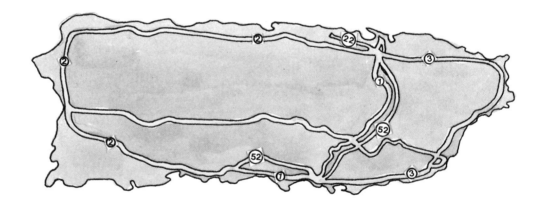

POPULATION DENSITY

Number of persons per square kilometer		Number of persons per square mile
more than 400		more than 1,000
300 to 400		750 to 1,000
200 to 300		500 to 750
Less than 200		Less than 500

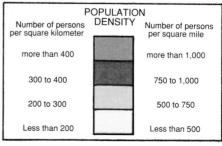

INDEX

Page numbers that appear in boldface type indicate illustrations

A woodcarver displaying his work

Roberto Clemente Stadium in Hato Rey

Picture Identifications
Front cover: Fort San Geronimo and the Condado district of San Juan
Pages 2-3: Cabo Rojo Lighthouse
Page 6: Doorway, old San Juan
Pages 8-9: Boquerón Beach on Puerto Rico's west coast
Pages 20-21: Montage of Puerto Rico residents
Page 28: El Morro
Pages 42-43: *Hacienda Aurora*, a painting of a nineteenth-century sugar plantation by
Francisco Oller
Page 56: The Puerto Rican and United States flags flying side by side in San Juan
Pages 80-81: Carnival in Ponce
Pages 92-93: A street in Old San Juan
Page 108: Montage of Puerto Rico symbols, including the flag, tree *(ceiba)*, bird *(reinita)*,
flower *(maga)*, and animal *(coquí)*
Page 137: Two elderly gentlemen taking a rest in San Germán
Back cover: Beach at Rincón

About the Author

Deborah Kent grew up in Little Falls, New Jersey, and received a Bachelor of Arts degree in English from Oberlin College. She earned a Masters degree in Social Work from Smith College School for Social Work, and worked for four years at the University Settlement House on New York's Lower East Side. She later moved to San Miguel de Allende, Mexico, where she began to write full-time.

Deborah Kent has published a dozen novels for young adults, as well as numerous titles in the *America the Beautiful* series. She lives in Chicago with her husband and their daughter Janna.

Picture Acknowledgments

Front cover, © Bob Glander/**SuperStock**; 2-3, © Bill Wassman/**APA Photo Agency**; 4, © Robert Frerck/**Odyssey/Frerck/Chicago**; 5, © W. Bertsch/**Fotoconcept, Inc.**; 6, © **Tony Arruza**; 8-9, © W. Bertşch/**H. Armstrong Roberts**; 11, © **Margo Taussig Pinkerton**; 12 (left), © **Mark Bacon**; 12 (right), © **Tony Arruza**; 13, © Bill Wassman/**APA Photo Agency**; 14, © W. Metzen/**H. Armstrong Roberts**; 15, (left), © John Curtis/**D. Donne Bryant Stock Photography Agency**; 15 (right), © Wally Hampton/**Marilyn Gartman Agency**; 16 (top left), © **Tony Arruza**; 16 (top right), © Bob Glander/**SuperStock**; 16 (bottom left), © E.R. Degginger/**H. Armstrong Roberts**; 16 (bottom right), © Al Tozer/**Stock Portfolio, Inc.**; 18, 19, © **Mark Bacon**; 20 (top left), © **Porterfield/Chickering**; 20 (bottom left), © **David R. Frazier Photolibrary**; 20 (bottom right), © Robert Frerck/**Odyssey/Frerck/Chicago**; 20 (top right), 21 (top right), © Suzanne L. Murphy/**D. Donne Bryant Stock Photography Agency**; 21 (top left), © Randa Bishop/**Tony Stone Worldwide, Chicago Ltd.**; 21 (bottom left, bottom right), © **Tony Arruza**; 23, 24 (two photos), © Suzanne L. Murphy/**D. Donne Bryant Stock Photography Agency**; 27, © **David R. Frazier Photolibrary**; 28, © Bill Wassman/**APA Photo Agency**; 30 (left), **Museum of History, Anthropology and Art of the University of Puerto Rico**; 30 (right), © **Mark Bacon**; 33, © W. Bertsch/**H. Armstrong Roberts**; 35, 36, 39 (right), **Historical Pictures Service, Chicago**; 39 (left), © **Chip & Rosa Maria Peterson**; 40, **La Casa del Libro, San Juan, Puerto Rico**; 42-43, **Collection of the Art Museum of the Americas/Audio Visual Program—O.A.S. Washington, D.C.**; 45, 46, **Museum of History, Anthropology and Art of the University of Puerto Rico**; 48, *Our Islands and Their People*; 49 (left), © **Chip & Rosa Maria Peterson**; 49 (right), **Museum of History, Anthropology and Art of the University of Puerto Rico**; 51, 52, 53, 55, *Our Islands and Their People*; 56, © **Mark Bacon**; 59 (left), *Our Islands and Their People*; 59 (right), **Archivo General de Puerto Rico**; 60, **AP/Wide World**; 62, **UPI/Bettmann**; 63 (left), **Archivo General de Puerto Rico**; 63 (right), **Independent Picture Service**; 64, **UPI/Bettmann**; 65, **Historical Pictures Service, Chicago**; 67, **AP/Wide World**; 68, 71, **UPI/Bettmann**; 72, © J. Messerschmidt/**H. Armstrong Roberts**; 75 (left), © **H. Armstrong Roberts**; 75 (right), © **David R. Frazier Photolibrary**; 76, © Bill Wassman/**APA Photo Agency**; 77, © **SuperStock**; 78, © Robert Frerck/**Tony Stone Worldwide/Chicago Ltd.**; 79, 80-81, © W. Bertsch/**Fotoconcept, Inc.**; 84 (two photos), **Museum of History, Anthropology and Art of the University of Puerto Rico**; 85, **Collection of the Art Museum of the Americas/Audio Visual Program—O.A.S. Washington, D.C.**; 86 (two photos), © **Mark Bacon**; 88, © **David R. Frazier Photolibrary**; 91, © W. Bertsch/**Fotoconcept**; 92-93, © **Tony Arruza**; 95, © Brian Parker/**Tom Stack & Associates**; 96 © Bill Wassman/**APA Photo Agency**; 97 (left), © Robert Frerck/**Odyssey/Frerck/Chicago**; 97 (right), © W. Bertsch/**Fotoconcept**; 98, © **David R. Frazier Photolibrary**; 99 (map), **Len Meents**; 99, 100, © Bill Wassman/**APA Photo Agency**; 101, © W. Metzen/**H. Armstrong Roberts**; 103 (left), © W. Bertsch/**H. Armstrong Roberts**; 103 (right), © **Mark Bacon**; 104, © **David R. Frazier Photolibrary**; 105, © Suzanne L. Murphy/**D. Donne Bryant Stock Photography Agency**; 105 (map), **Len Meents**; 107, 108 (tree), © Robert Frerck/**Odyssey/Frerck/Chicago**; 108 (flag), **Courtesy Flag Research Center, Winchester, MA 01890**; 108 (bird), © **Dr. Robert Ross**; 108 (frog, flower), © **Mark Bacon**; 112, © W. Bertsch/**H. Armstrong Roberts**; 113, © Larry Lipsky/**Tom Stack & Associates**; 114, © **David R. Frazier Photolibrary**; 115, © **Photri**; 117, © **Porterfield/Chickering**; 118 (two photos), © **Puerto Rico Tourism Company**; 120, © Robert Frerck/**Odyssey/Frerck/Chicago**; 121, © **SuperStock**; 123, *Our Islands and Their People*; 125 (Campos), **AP/Wide World**; 125 (Alonso), **Archivo General de Puerto Rico**; 126 (Badillo, Betancourt, Casals), **AP/Wide World**; 126 (Betances), 127 (Cestero), **Archivo General de Puerto Rico**; 127 (Clemente, Columbus, Cruz), 128 (Feliciano, Ferré, Ferrer), **AP/Wide World**; 128 (Diego), 129 (Lopez, Marqués), **Archivo General de Puerto Rico**; 129 (Meléndez), © **José Sanchez**; 129 (Julia), 130 (Moreno, Munoz Marín, Padilla), **AP/Wide World**; 130 (Paoli), **Archivo General de Puerto Rico**; 131 (Ponce de León), **Historical Pictures Service, Chicago**; 131 (Puente) **AP/Wide World**; 131 (Quiñones, Rincón), **Archivo General de Puerto Rico**; 132 (Stahl), © **José Sanchez**; 132 (Gandía), **Archivo General de Puerto Rico**; 136 (maps), **Len Meents**; 138 © Suzanne L. Murphy/**D. Donne Bryant Stock Photography Agency**; 141, 143, © Bill Wassman/**APA Photo Agency**; back cover, © Al Tozer/**Stock Portfolio, Inc.**